SHAKIM BIO PRESENTS

Loyalty, Honor & Respect

The sequel to Love, Hell or Right

LOYALTY, HONOR & RESPECT

Copyright © 2016 Shakim Bio

Written by: Shakim Bio

Edited by: Greg Martin

Cover photo: Ced Killings

Cover art and design: Greg Martin

Published With Permission by Mikahs 7 Publishing

ISBN: 978-0-9846596-2-3

First Edition

Also by ShaKim Bio -

"Love, Hell or Right" - The very 1st God & Earth love story

"The Last Illest" - The 1st official Street-Hop novel

I don't shoot guns no more... I shoot ink!

Acknowledgements

Peace and love to my Day 1 family that's been there for me from Day 1 always supporting me and having my back no matter what [you know who you be!!] Greg 'G' Ali/G. Millz Martin... Always there... Ms. Sonya Yeargin... my mother, Ms. Cynthia Guice and the Guice/Brown Family. Peace to the Nation of Gods & Earths... All the Gods I ever built with past, present, and future. Peace to the Five Percenter newspaper and staff.

G. Kalim and Born King. To my seeds DaQuan Original and Shamel. To Oceasia Divine True Earth, my young diva Evher Peace and the Tanner Family... much love to 'Beauty'... much love to Ms. Pam Quigley at Book Gang Media for everything you shared with me. To Ashe Bandele... to Seth 'Soulman' Ferranti and Diane at Gorilla Convict Publications for everything... Sparro aka Larry Williams, Junta Entertainment New Me Movement. Al Monday, Benson, Len God, Tiz, Spice, Cee Reality, ShaBorn, Kamel [Rich Kid]. Kelly Blue.

To all my brothers and comrades caught up in the struggle and still at war... Don't stop... Can't stop... and to all the women who stand by us and hold us down, uplift us, inspire us, motivate us and never hold us back... much love for overstanding this struggle and still willing to love us and be there... Kevin Gray [D.C.], Detroit Turk... Blackhand Publishing. Blast, Cheeks, Shameek, Emile Dixon, Hoffa, B.K., Lou Simms, Star, Qasim, Junglist.

"Rest in Peace to Maurice "Skinny Moe" Fields," Kenneth "Ken Low" Hill," Garland "S.I." Tyree," and those brothers who made it home for the year 2015, but did not live to see the year 2016.

To all my peeps from all over I didn't forget you. Too many to name.

To all the ones who claimed to have my back and said they will support the movement but didn't live up to their word, dropped the ball, or didn't even buy a novel… It's still all love… I still refuse to fail or lose…

I looked at all that I needed in life…

and all that I wanted…

and all that I was given in life…

and realized that life is too beautiful and too short

to accept less than my worth.

Love,

Hell

or

Right

The very 1st God & Earth love story

CHAPTER 1

I remember sitting in Marion Supermax prison in 2000. I was sent there with about twenty other convicts on an emergency transfer over some drama that popped off in U.S.P. Terre Haute.

While I was there, which was for a very short period, I met some real good brothers who were part of the struggle, but were just trapped off. I had a correspondence approval with one of my co-defendants, who, was in another institution. I told him that I was transferred to the well-known and notorious supermax... and while there, I caught an incident report for being in possession of a sharpened instrument [homemade knife] so I was in the hole. My codefendant sent me a package. It was a Xerox copy of a book he found in the law library. He sent it to me like it was law work material. It was "The Prisoner's Wife" by Asha Bandele.

The novel was about a black woman who was a student in college and who, as a favor for a friend, volunteered to read her poetry to a group of prisoners during a Black History Month program. It was on that trip that she met a man who was imprisoned there for murder. That man was to become her boyfriend, her confidante, her husband, her lover and soul mate. That novel was very touching to me because I was in prison and could relate. I'd never known of or read a story like that. I read it in 24 hours.

After reading the novel, I shared it with the rest of convicts on the tier. The whole tier read that Xerox version of The Prisoner's Wife, and that novel sparked big interesting debates among us. We spoke on how we'd seen and understood that story about their love and the hardships they went through.

We sat up from the late night hours to the early mornings telling stories of our encounters with our girls, wives, baby mothers, those that stayed and those that left us.

At that particular time, I was still in touch and in tune with a couple females. I did not have a girl that I was thinking about building a future with. I writing all kinds of letters back and forth with Tammi and Oceasia and I exchanged maybe two letters and we were only dealing with building on mathematics and our culture, but still I felt Ashe's story because now I was in the same environment as the character, Rashid, from her story. I was now incarcerated in prison with time in the spaceship / football numbers to do and I now realized I took a lot of the simplest things in life for granted... one of them being the female.

As years went by, my communication with females grew... some were very short lived and some were fruitful, but still I didn't see myself building a future with any one particular female.

In 2004, when Oceasia and I were communicating again, it was something that was meant to be. I look at things from all angles. I was in the box [again] pending "under investigation" and needed to get my mind back right and on point. Oceasia, at that time, was going through a lot on her end. So for us to lose communication and link back like that at a time where we both needed it the most was proof that mathematics do not lie and it was meant to be.

I always kept *The Prisoner's Wife* story in a class by itself. I appreciated that story because I was in prison and could see and feel what the characters in the story were going through and after experiencing what I did with Oceasia, I knew and overstood similar hardships. When I came up with the idea to write *Love, Hell or Right*, I came from not only what I was and still go through, but what every man in prison is going through as well. I was just man enough to express my emotional state and speak on those issues, when just about every man, who writes a book, writes about the love of the game and the things that come with it.

Being a God centered, cultured man, who is a member of the Nation of Gods and Earths, I wanted to come different and produce the very first God and Earth love novel in print, which I did. I wanted to be the first to bring something of value to the open public as well as my love for my woman. I also tried to target three audiences with Love, Hell or Right... 1) the Nation of Gods and Earths... I wanted us to have a story that was ours; 2) women... especially the ones who are going through the hardships and struggles of loving a man in prison; and 3) the brothers, who were in this stuggle and going through the same thing with woman on the outside. I felt I did a great job of sharing my story, but I didn't do such a great job of balancing the audiences that I targeted. A lot of people criticized the novel before even reading it. The cover artwork included the universal flag and that alone put a stigma on the novel from the start. The universal flag made a lot of people pass on the novel. It was barred out of a few state prisons. I promoted and marketed it by advertising in the Five Percenter newspaper, and I was given great support. I paid for a four-month ad on the back page of the paper... unfortunately I did not make a lot of sales. I sent two-sided fliers to all Allah Youth Centers and schools all over the country. Had the novel everywhere the Gods & Earths frequented... but the sales were still low. A lot of my sales were from brothers who were incarcerated.

9

What I needed was a promotional push. I tried to get someone to come aboard and help me out. I spent a lot of money in the process. I did get RaeKwon from Wu-Tang to take a photo holding up the novel, Rapper A.Z The Visualizer, basketball star Carmelo Anthony also took a photo with the novel, and superstar singer Alicia Keys did support my cause by buying a copy of the novel. I also tried to get Mary J. Blige and others to promote the novel. I gave away a lot of free novels.

Most women who read the novel loved it. They all said the same thing; that it started out slow and they got lost with the back and forth building of mathematics in ciphers until the novel picked up between me and Oceasia. Then they couldn't put the book down. A few people reached out to me and told me that they really appreciated the novel. To me, that was enough confirmation of a job very well done. I did get the constructive criticism from my convict peers. Some claiming that the Nation of Gods & Earths is not building like that nowadays and that lost a lot of people, especially putting the universal flag on the cover's artwork. But overall, I was saluted for my work on my first published novel.

One of my Jamaican bredden confided in me and told me that his girl bought the novel and at first was lost with the 'God-body talk' but she forced herself through the powerful science that was being dropped and once she got passed it, she couldn't put the novel down. It made her laugh. It made her cry. She loved the story. She felt the love I have for my Earth. He told me that my novel caused a debate between he and his girl but she got a better overstanding of what we go through. He told me this after he'd gotten a visit [the novel was a hot topic]. He said my book also caused an argument because I put too much out there but his

10

girl said she could tell I love my girl and my girl should cherish and appreciate me for that.

I sometimes question if my Earth cherishes or appreciates me for that. Why I say that? The novel was a hot topic and like I stated earlier, I wasn't getting no real push. Oceasia, out of everyone, should have been pushing me as well as the novel. She out of all people should have wanted the novel to do well. I thought that she would have taken the steering wheel and made sure that our novel was on every social media platform. I'm in no way trying to put any blame on her... the sales were low and still may have produced the same results even with her doing more to help. It's just that I didn't see her trying to do anything when I felt she should have been my greatest push.

The sales coming from the Five Percenter newspaper were low. The novel just didn't do what was expected. I thought it would have moved at a terrific speed. It was poorly marketed and promoted, and not supported. Born u truth [But] I am still standing tall and still spraying ink. I still felt it was worth a sequel titled *Loyalty, Honor & Respect.*

My purpose of this sequel wasn't to let everyone know the status of me and Oceasia's relationship, it's to open the eyes of those who recognize real love and overstand the struggle of a woman who loves a man who is locked up in prison. I want to give strength to both the males and females involved. This is not just my story because its personal... it's a story that involves both individuals because I am not the only one who is going through this. There are millions who are in this same position. I just chose to share my story.

I could have tried to use my story to exploit my culture... or I could have come from another angle and tried to recreate a "50 Shades of Grey" type of novel but being on some pervert shit would have disrespected the true and living God that I am and represent. Maybe the novel *Love, Hell or Right* would have been a best seller and still on USA Today's [newspaper] Top 50 books list but being true to myself, I did not do that. I shared personal letters and poems that I wrote to my Earth and her responses, her personal poems and songs she did for me. I shared our hardships and all. I kept it official... all the way.

Everyone always asks me "What's up with Oceasia?"... "Are y'all still together?"... "Did y'all get married yet?"

Well, I'm going to tell the story of what happened and where we at and where we stand.

"Woman"

Raheem DeVaughn

I sometimes wonder where Raheem DeVaughn's mind was when he wrote the words to that song... or when he sang that song. That song is beautiful. It makes me feel great and I start thinking about all women... How beautiful they really are... How special they are... I miss every little detail about a woman. I start to really appreciate my sons' mothers... My mother... All my sisters... My aunts... female cousins... nieces. I start thinking about all the bullshit I put females through. I miss holding a woman... making love to her... making her moan and scream my name... bringing her to the greatest climax she ever had... I miss waking up to her [any woman], coming home to her [any woman]. I miss walking in the malls and seeing women everywhere... looking so sexy... playing hard to get... I miss the educated woman... the highly intelligent woman... the not so smart woman. I miss all women. No matter their shape, size, color or nationality, height, shoe size, hair color, hair length, hair style... I miss all of that, their voice, their smiles, their loving and caring ways... their attitudes... The way they make me feel.

Everything.

I can't wait to go home to always be there with my woman, making her feel special, showing her that she really means the world to me...

...That she is my woman.

Loyalty Honor and Respect

"I'm an outlaw… got an outlaw chick / Bumping 2 Pac on
my outlaw shit"

Jay-Z featuring Beyonce

"On the run part II"

15

CHAPTER 2

Every convict in prison dreams of having the ultimate chick... that superwoman that takes care of everything and holds him down. In these times, women are not looking for lame ass men who can't handle their business while taking care of house and home. That's also how dudes in prison, view women... we don't want no bum ass chick who can't take care of business. These days, women have even bigger positions in life. No more housewife or just being mom... women are obtaining degrees and displaying their professionalism and skills on extraordinary levels; they move quickly up the ranks wherever they're employed, they are CEO's of big corporations or they own their own companies. Shit, these days, many women are making six or seven figure salaries and are the breadwinners of their households. These women have great vision and potential. I mean it's cool to vibe with a street oriented chick or hood type chick but we're talking about building a future at some point. Don't get me wrong. I love street chicks, their attitudes, aggressiveness and all that, but I need a woman who has vision, is about her business and about her man, of course. My thing is, "if a woman isn't holding her man down... then she's holding him back." I don't need a woman holding me back. My woman is supposed to have my back... she should push me to do better, be better, she be my motivation and my inspiration. Now that might sound crazy coming from me, being that I'm here in prison but truthfully, I'm surrounded by concrete and steel bars but the only thing about me that is limited and contained is my physical being and that still can't stop my mental or spiritual self. I'm going to be my woman's motivation. I'm going to have her back no matter what. I can overlook a lot of small things because I can see the overall picture that she and I envision.

All of that is not as easy as it reads or sounds, especially for a man in prison, the woman, as well as the man, experience hardships. Some women refuse to deal with those or any hardships of bidding with (sticking with for the duration of a prison sentence) a man in prison. **I know it is hard**. I spoke on some of these hardships in *Love, Hell or Right,* the prequel to this novel. We all want a female that is trustworthy, loyal and faithful... and that's asking for a whole lot cause I mean, look where we are... Prison.

I know no matter how mentally strong or how much will power a woman may appear to have, she is still a woman and women are emotional. My woman is gonna need to be held, loved so eventually she will need that physical, intimate attention [sex] and being locked up, I cannot give that to her, which becomes a very big obstacle for us as it does in any relationship between a man who is in prison and a woman who is in the free world. The man cannot be a full provider because he cannot provide her physical and sexual needs. Some get through these phases better than others, or better than most... phone sex is cool. I enjoy phone sex with my girl... hearing her please herself and screaming my name and so on... but it takes more than that... the phone calls are limited, no matter how many phone lines you got secured or how many times you call back. After a while it gets played out and a woman is going to want the real thing... the foreplay, the actual session and all the laying up and cuddling after the fact. So sometimes all that phone sex is doing is making her more horny and opening doors for other stuff that requires her to seek that physical attention. That's a harsh reality... some of us cannot accept that.

There are so many obstacles and hardships that come with loving a man or woman who is in prison but love is such a beautiful thing... one of the greatest feelings ever. One can never say what they would or wouldn't do because once love is involved, everything changes. I'm speaking on how some women say they could never deal with a man in prison and how a man in prison can't do anything for them... in the long run, these are the same women who fall in love and love us the hardest.

Some think that men in prison got game because most of us got ourselves well put together in many aspects and are on point but I said most of us... not all of us, for some of us ARE full of game. Prison is a fucked up place, it's the lowest level of society, inhabited by some of the worst individuals, who are labeled criminals. There are a lot of people in prison that truly belong there for the crimes that they committed but there are also a great-deal of people who don't belong there. In prison, there are some people, who have really changed for their own benefit and for the benefit of society. There are men in prison with great family values, morals, principles, and character, amongst other great values. Some of these men are hard workers and future teachers, leaders, and guides to our youth, some are universal builders and some destroyers but for a better world of tomorrow.

Women do see these qualities and potential in us... this is why they are with us now, some we meet while in prison doing our bid and others we know from when we were out there free.

Some women don't understand why other women choose to deal with us. They say, *"He's in jail... what can he do for you?"* To them, the thought of dealing with a man in prison is crazy and any female who has a relationship with a man who is locked up, is out of her mind. *"What I look like claiming a man who is in jail?* [Is what she says]" This is the same man, who when he was out on free land, made things happen that created opportunities for others to eat, make money and take care of their families. Men, who when they were at the top of their game, these same woman would do just about anything just to get near them or to get their time and attention.

There are countless women, who refuse to deal with or bid with a man, who ends up in prison, but when that man was free, these women were well taken care of and reaped the benefits of the crimes that spoiled them with luxury before that man was incarcerated. All women have brothers, cousins, uncles, fathers, husbands, fiancés, boyfriends or some male friend, who has either a family member or associate that is in prison. Prison life affects just about everyone. Can you honestly say you don't know of anyone who has been locked up? Everybody deserves love. You want someone to love and care about you, right? So what makes it so wrong or crazy for an incarcerated man to want the same thing? What if it was your father or your brother who went to prison, would you turn your back and abandon him? Would you be there for him to inspire and keep him strong? Would you encourage his woman to stay with him and hold him down, bring the kids or keep his children in their Dad's life? What if it were you who was in prison... wouldn't you want someone to be there for you?

I've met a lot of women who claimed they wouldn't give a man in prison the time of day but after some phone conversations and they really got to know me personally, they started liking my character and my energy. Even if we never move on to any other status, they were willing to give me their time to converse, laugh and we enjoyed each other's company, even if it was just a 15 minute phone call. I can be that ear when you just need someone there who will listen. I can be the one with good advice, a solution or I can be the one who inspires you to do better and be better. It doesn't have to be me, it can be any man who is in prison and it doesn't always have to end up as a relationship. It can be a friendship. A woman might inspire that man to go to church and change his life or inspire him to be a better father to his children and a better person to their mother. A woman can awaken something in a man that he didn't see before causing him to appreciate women. After that, he just might go back to his girl, baby-mother or wife as a better man. You never know what you can do for someone. Just like you never know what he can do for you. There are so many women raising sons without father at home. That man in prison can be a father figure from behind bars. He can still teach a boy how to be a man and alert him to pitfalls he should avoid in life. He knows and understands about peer pressure and how one wants to be down and accepted, the influences of the world and certain cultures that lead our youth into negativity and to prison.

A man in prison can still make a difference. How many women can admit that they have been pampered by a man? What about having very intellectual conversations? It can be about politics, family structure, science, world news, nature or relationships with men in general. Men in prison are masters in all

20

fields. We have time to read, research, and study. We do what we can to enhance our minds, bodies, and soul. We work out hard. Women are attracted to the way we look, some of us are well defined with big biceps, broad shoulders and big chests... chiseled abs... nice strong legs... they way we bare tattoos... some with stories being told by just looking at them. How we keep up with perfect hygiene... white teeth, always smelling good, the waves in our hair got them seasick or the nice clean dreads and we keep the perfectly lined up facial hairs. Despite the bars between us, women still find themselves attracted to the way we carry ourselves, the way we walk, talk, how intellectual we are or how gangster we seem to be. There is something that they are attracted too. You should see the gleam in my girl's eyes when I walk into that visiting room. She isn't the only one who sees it and takes notice... everyone does. They turn their heads to look and see who that is who just entered the room. My strong energy is felt like that. I'm not the only one like that. A lot of men in prison feel that way. I know that I'm a better individual than I was and I've made progress out of my situation. I educated myself and taken advantage of the things that were made available to me. I learned to make great lemonade out of the batch of lemons I was given. I have to remain a General and stand tall.

Every man must be a man and accept responsibility of being one. Whether that responsibility is being a father, husband... whatever, we still have to respect and honor that title and live up to it.

So with that being said... y'all women need to stop trying to shit on us. Even though we still have flaws, most of us are striving to get ourselves together.

"Fool for You"

Ceelo Green featuring Melanie Fiona

CHAPTER 3

Many people who read *Love, Hell or Right* felt that I was a fool to accept Oceasia back and choosing her over Tammi. The novel was made to cause debates... how I felt was how I felt. You might feel otherwise if you were in that situation. Some people move with their minds, others move with their hearts. Some people move with what they feel is right for them so that makes this topic debatable for everyone. I felt I did right. Now, do I feel I made the right or wrong decision? That question sometimes comes to mind. Why? Because either way, there still would have been ups and downs, trials and tribulations, pleasure and pain, victories and struggles. That's what relationships are all about, they're never all peaches and cream... plus the fact that I am in prison complicates some issues.

One of the things Oceasia and I had in common was our culture. Outside of that, we had a lot more in common and we were very compatible. Tammi and I had several things in common as well and we were compatible but we did not have the same culture. That made me see Oceasia in a different light even though she was not living out her culture and knew better, I still chose her.   Since then, a lot has transpired and a lot of things have changed but overall, I was still with her... maybe because I was a fool for her but a fool isn't always a fool all the time. Sometimes a fool becomes the wiser... remember, a wise man can play the role of a fool but a fool can never play the role of a wise man.

"No Mediocre"

T.I. featuring Iggy Azalea

I've been locked up for a very long time but I don't think my taste in women has changed, however, my standards are not the same. I am not a television watcher but I may be walking towards the microwave to cook something or on my way to the computers and I'll look up in the direction of the TV's [there are approximately 7 to 8 TV's in the unit so you can't miss seeing one or glance at what's on the screen. The beauty I be seeing on there sometimes stops me in my tracks where I have to look and ask, "Yo, who is that?" There are so many reality shows and programs that feature some very attractive women. I can't wait to get home and just be in the constant presence of women or just one woman.

Reality shows like "Basketball Wives," "Love and Hip Hop," "Bad Girls of Atlanta," or "Bad Girls of Miami," and many more... the women on those shows are beautiful, there is no denying that. Most of these R&B singers are awesome... Have you seen what Jennifer Hudson looks like nowadays? How about Keyshia Cole or K Michelle? Seeing the drama Keyshia Cole is going through with her husband, Daniel 'Boobie' Gibson will make you think about your situation. Kinda makes you feel like you could love her completely and dedicate your life to her and her only. You speak on how you would not have done her wrong. Everybody has a version of what they would or wouldn't do but the reality of it is you are only speaking like that because you are locked up. You don't know what you would have done. You would have been just as arrogant and stupid as any man in that position who is living that life. There are so many women out there to choose from, prison just changes your views and how you think while you're behind the bars.

It's a few industry chicks I be checking for that I'm feeling based solely on their looks. I like Tika Sumpter out of so many others. I feel if I was out there in the free world, those same women would be feeling me and wanting to get at me. I'm not going to lie or front... those shorties be looking so good on TV. Got me missing them like crazy!! It makes me appreciate and cherish women even more and I'm so grateful for what I have. That's why I hold onto mine so hard. I see how some of these men drool and wish that they had someone to love or love them back or even be in a position to get that kind of love. Picture Keyshia Cole or even K. Michelle singing love songs to you about how much she loves you or how much you are hurting her. Men on the street may laugh on how men in prison start feeling emotional like, "Damn, I wish I was the one shorty was talking to."

Just simple looking shorties like Melanie Fiona are so beautiful. The sisters of Hip Hop got a reality show and those women on there look more than decent and I don't hardly even watch television born u truth [but] I like to look at the beauty of women... women are what makes a man complete, she is secondary but very much necessary. I love women who are very independent and work hard for theirs... a woman who has objectives, life goals and very high aims. I can't see myself with a woman who has no goals. I refuse to go that route. I've been there too many times before while I was in the free world and in prison. I don't need a trailer load of women. All I need is one chick and nah, she won't be no mediocre chick either.

Mona Scott-Young, who is an executive producer of one of those reality shows is a beautiful, independent sister. She is not sitting at home waiting for no man to take care of her. She is out there grinding just as hard.

"Arm - Leg - Leg - Arm - Head / This is GodBody"

"Heaven"

Jay-Z

CHAPTER 4

There was a lot of controversy and negative talk going on when Hip Hop superstar Jay-Z was seen wearing a gold chain with the universal flag on a pendant encrusted with diamonds while he was sitting on the sidelines of an NBA game with his wife, Beyonce'. There was even crazy backlash from the Gods and Earths (men and women of the Five Percent Nation) behind Jay-Z wearing the flag... some felt that he shouldn't wear it since he isn't a member of the Nation of Gods & Earths. There were great builds in the Five Percenter newspaper about when the universal flag was designed by Universal Shamgaud in 1966 and they were put on pendants. The Father Allah started passing them out in 1967 to a lot of his associates, who didn't have knowledge of self, and when asked why he was giving the pendants away to non-members and his response was "You don't know how far one person can take the flag."

Jay-Z is the biggest superstar in Hip Hop and as a person he is a corporation. He is a business. His wearing the universal flag of Islam was / is an honor. He can take the flag where a lot of Gods and Earths can't go. He is called "The God of Flow." Just him alone wearing the flag opened doors for the younger generation and people who are curious as to who the Nation of Gods and Earths are and what we represent. This is where and when the universal builders should have been on the scene to show and prove. You got the greatest emcee in Hip Hop... or should I say the biggest emcee in Hip Hop wearing and representing our flag and you want to complain? I wish I was out so I could have pushed Love, Hell or Right , even harder after that.

Jay-Z is from Brooklyn, New York and came up in the era when Gods were on every corner and schoolyard. In the 80's and early 90's, the Nations influence was everywhere in New York, you could not escape it so of course Jay-Z was impacted by it. Supreme Mathematics and the Supreme Alphabets affected everyone in that era. The Gods were everywhere in New York City. I felt honored the first time Born Justice, who later changed his name attribute to Kashon, pinned the universal flag pendant on my shirt, back in 1983. Born Justice gave the whole neighborhood knowledge of self and his students, in turn, had students. I was one of his "first-born" student's students. I knew 120 lessons maybe a few days after my enlightener back in 1981. I was 11-years-old and I was able to show and prove and break down the universal flag from every point and angle. I was going on 13-years-old, meaning I was still 12 when he gave me my first flag. I felt like I was given a Grammy. It's been close to 30 years and I've had so many flags since then. I now have the universal flag tatted on the left side of my upper chest.

Supreme Mathematics and Supreme Alphabets still affect everyone around me.

I noticed Wise and AB on the yard, watching convicts run a full court, five on five, game. Some of these convicts play hard like they're in the NBA... like they're not doing a million years in the United States Federal Penitentiary, Coleman II prison. Playing basketball was some of these convicts' lives and their reality. I'd been at Coleman II for close to five years at the time. Wise and

30

"AB God" were there before me. When I first arrived from USP Big Sandy, they greeted me and I met the God Divine, who was an elder God from Panama, but was raised in Brooklyn and months later the God JahKee, who is from Boston, arrived on the prison compound. We were the five universal builders on that compound. There were other God-bodies there but we were the ones always on the scene building and showing and proving. We kept the ciphers going.

Wise and I stayed battling it out with the lessons. Wise was a brown-skinned understanding seed... meaning he was light-skinned but also brown-skinned... he was a light brown-skinned brother, about five feet, eleven inches tall and a little overweight. He weighed 220 lbs. He use to box and talk about his vicious training but was lazy on the vicious work out. He was about 29-years-old with a 40-year sentence.

"AB God" was a slim wisdom seed, meaning he was brown-skinned. He was very slim in build but was toned up. He worked out every morning from 6am until 2pm. He had dreads down his back; clean, thin dreads that he kept in a Rasta looking crown but was in very great shape. Just by looking at him, no one could ever guess his age. "AB" was six feet tall and weighed about 140 lbs. He was from Newburgh, New York and Wise was from Norfolk, Virginia but when they spoke, it always pertained to Mathematics or the universal language of the Nation of Gods and Earths. As I approached them, they both stood to give me a pound (handshake) and half embrace.

"Peace to the God!!" said AB God.

"Peace God!" said Wise.

"Knowledge-knowledge!" I replied.

For the Gods who are on point with their lessons "Knowledge-Knowledge" is one-one or eleven... the eleventh degree in the Twelve Jewels of Islam is 'Peace' so I used the supreme mathematics to say 'peace.'

I sat down on the grey, metal bleacher as Wise and AB God sat back down.

"What's the science Blackman?" I asked.

"Always constant elevation ShaKim... Always," said AB.

"True indeed," I added as Wise nodded his head in agreement.

The weather in central Florida was amazing. It was nice and warm outside and it was only late February. I was dressed in a pair of grey, Russell sweatpants with a pair of black and white Nike "Hyper-fusion" basketball sneakers and a thick, grey t-shirt ... my broad chest and eighteen and a half inch arms were still outlined in the shirt and even though the shirt was one size too big, my six day workout was very apparent. I'm a 5 feet 10 inch 190 pound, wisdom seed [brown-skinned] bald headed, street and penitentiary General.

Wise was wearing his institutional brown khaki pants with a pair of black Timberland boots. He had on a thick, zip-up grey sweatshirt with the collar even though the weather did not call for the sweat jacket. AB God was wearing some cargo shorts made out of the industrial khaki pants with the big pockets and a pair of shell-toe Adidas sneakers that he kept in great condition. He also had on a crispy, short-sleeved, white t-shirt as well as his crown with the tassel. AB was a very old school God and laid back.

As convicts ran up and down the basketball court displaying their skills, there were a couple of slam dunks here and there, as we sat back watching the game while holding our own conversations.

"Yo, Bio... How is the Earth doing God?" AB God asked me.

"She is peace... We built earlier today. Everything is good with her," I   replied.

"How is young Earth Evher doing?" he asked.

"She is real peace also... she is so intelligent... she's in a gifted class and everything." I stayed bragging about "Evher Peace", who is Oceasia's daughter; at barely 7-years-old, she already knew her Supreme Math and Supreme Alphabets. She was also getting significant modeling work, was was already featured in a Nordstrom's catalog and was learning ballet and karate. I was so proud of Evher, who I called "My Young Diva."

"That's peace God. I'm glad that everything is love within your cipher with your family," spoke AB.

"True indeed," I responded.

"Yo, ShaKim Bio let me ask your understanding on some things," said Wise.

"What's the science Wise?"

I turned toward him waiting for his question.

"When you were given your Supreme Mathematics... once you had them on cap... did you have to "born" them out yourself or were they already "borned" out when you got them?"

"I had to born them out myself,"

"Ok," said AB. "At what stage in your obtaining 120 did you start borning them out?" AB asked.

"Hmmmmm," I thought as I put my finger to my chin and tried to recall when I learned how to born words.

"Borning" is when you take any word then take each letter from the alphabet, which is 1 through 26 and you use the number of the alphabet to convert the letters to numbers and add the total numbers up. If the total comes to a double-digit number, you then add those 2 numbers until it comes to a one digit total. For instance, "knowledge" is the first degree in the Supreme Mathematics, so you take the letters and convert them into numbers k is the 11th letter, N is the 14th, O is the 15th, W is the 23rd, L is the 12th, E is the 5th, D is the 4th, G is the 7th and E is the 5th. You add it up... 11+14+15+23+12+5+4+7+5 = 96. 9+6 = 15 and 1+5 = 6 in the Supreme Mathematics is Equality, so knowledge "borns" equality.

You then have to be able to show not only mathematically but through the science of life itself, how knowledge "borns" equality. That was the uniqueness of Mathematics. You had to be swift and changeable. It wasn't about being able to quote degrees.

You had to be able to break them down to the simplest form then show and prove.

"I started "borning" things out like right after I "knowledged" the Twelve Jewels of Islam," I told both AB God and Wise. "See I was given Supreme Mathematics one degree at a time. I had to be able to quote that degree before I was given the next one... After a while, I was taught how to born things out... the first thing I had to born out was my attribute... from there, I moved to other things like the math, Alphabets and so on" I spoke with certainty.

"So you wasn't borning out your attribute from the very beginning?" Wise asked.

"Now Cipher [No]... I didn't know how and wasn't able to show and prove at that stage... I wasn't given an attribute until after I knew the Supreme Mathematics. I was taught and groomed by Elder Gods who taught Gods, who were a just few years older than me," I replied.

"Wise got a student in the unit who he has borning out his attribute, born u truth [but] he can't even quote Supreme Math or Alphabets on point yet," AB interjected.

"So he can't really show and prove" I finished off for him.

"Exactly," said AB God.

"Nah... Wise, you have to take baby steps with him" I added.

"Now Cipher! He is not a little boy. He is a grown man," said Wise. "My Enlightener gave me my lessons all at once from the attribute stage to math all the way to the solar facts. I had to learn on my own."

"That still doesn't make it right and exact to do that to your student," AB argued.

"I'm not... I'm just advancing him now," said Wise as we laughed at him.

"Ahite, ShaKim Bio... since everybody's always run to you concerning lessons and showing and proving, do you know the Supreme Mathematics, borned? Can you tell me knowledge to cipher right here and now?" as Wise smirked his game face smirks. That's Wise for you... always challenging somebody, especially me. We stayed at it. He wanted to make sure I was as sharp and swift as everyone always claims I am.

"Maaan, that's a good one," says AB God, who was always doing what he did when Wise challenged me. "I know Sha should be able to do that... ain't that true God?" he asked me.

"The Supreme Mathematics borned?" I repeat the question. I looked at my watch, which read 1:40 pm. We had one hour and 20 minutes before yard recall and I knew I could add math with the quickness... especially the ones I didn't recall off hand. As I rubbed my chin again, I asked "How you want it?... From its total to its grand total or what?"

"You can just give me the all being born to total... make it easy on yourself," responded Wise, as he got a laugh out of both AB God and I.

"That makes it even easier for the Bio-Chemical Wise one," suggested AB.

"Knowledge borns equality... Wisdom borns build understanding borning knowledge-knowledge, which is all being born to wisdom," I stated.

"You don't have to give me the full breakdown," said Wise.

"Well, nothing was ever given to me easy, other than all this Fed time I have," I shot back. "Understanding borns knowledge power cipher borning equality, culture borns knowledge, freedom borns equality, equality borns knowledge wisdom all being born to understanding," I proclaimed as I thought out the next degree.

"Power borns God God which borns knowledge culture all being born to power or refinement... refinement borns knowledge cipher born all being born to knowledge. Equality borns Knowledge-Knowledge cipher all being born to wisdom," as I looked up in the clear blue sky. "God borns wisdom equality all being born to Build or Destroy."

"That should have been real easy," said AB God, who was encouraging the challenge, knowing I am swift enough to add up and get everything on point.

"Build borns culture build borning knowledge wisdom all being born to understanding. Destroy borns knowledge cipher equality all being born to God."

I sat back calculating the next degree as Wise sat still with his smirk.

"Born borns culture born borning knowledge understanding all being born to culture or freedom and cipher borns power born borning knowledge culture freedom all being born to power or refinement."

Wise put his fist out to give me a pound, AB God did too, after Wise.

"ShaKim... I respect that about you. You sat here and borned the Supreme Math and you even added it up in your mentals" Wise acknowledged.

"That was nothing to me... we can show and prove mathematically dealing with today's reality on how and why they born that nowadays if you want," I said.

"That's Right!!" shouted AB God.

"Then we can do that with the Supreme Alphabets... and the Twelve Jewels," I added.

"True indeed," spoke AB again.

"And if we have adding problems... we can get a pen or pencil and paper to make sure we got everything right and exact... Matter fact let's begin now... You do one and I do the next and AB follows... we are going to start with the

Supreme Alphabets," I instructed Wise. "Yeah, we can start now and wherever we leave off, we can come out after the culture hour count [4pm] and continue."

I advised as Wise still sats there with that funny smirk on his face.

"If Its Love"

Kem featuring Chrisette Michelle

CHAPTER 5

"Bredden... wha di bloodclot gwaan?... You crazy or something?" This is what my Jamaican partner said to me when he came looking for me in the housing unit and couldn't find me. After questioning others as to where I might be, he finally found me in the Mexican's cell sitting across from the Mexican in a chair. He couldn't believe I was there. The Mexican was a tattoo artist and he was doing a tattoo design that we had been working on for a few days. Now, I was actually getting a tattoo in his cell.

At first, the Mexican artist was drawing up my Mikahs 7 Publishing logo for me and after getting my vision on paper exactly how I wanted it, he asked me if I wanted a tattoo. I already had one tattoo, which was the universal flag on the left side of my chest. I really wasn't tryna go through all that pain of getting another one but I told him I would get with him in a couple days. Next thing you know, I was going through the different patterns of the alphabet letters he had... I searched through the curvy designs and fancy letters until I found exactly what I wanted. He drew it up and had everything perfect. I just had to find the time and courage to go through with it.

I was getting Oceasia's name tatted on me so when my Jamaican partner came in the "tattoo cell" and saw what I was doing, he thought I was crazy. I was getting Oceasia's name tatted on my right hand vertically between my pinky finger and wrist... right there on the side of my hand with designs and all. It was painful and it took a few days, then it had to heal, then I had to get it done over and over to make sure it was set in right. I'm right handed and always using that hand so once everything healed, I

41

got it outlined in red ink so it stood out even more. I was repping the woman I loved to the fullest.

"Yo B... yu gwaan mad... shorty got you repping her like that?... Wowww!!!" was his response as he shook his head and started laughing at me.

"Yeah sun... I'm crazy all right," I shot back at him, as I went through the pain of getting tatted.

A few weeks passed and I didn't tell Oceasia about the tattoo during our daily phone calls. While I was on a visit with my partner 'G', who flew in from New York, he questioned me about the tattoo he saw on my hand.

"Yo, Sha... What's that?" G asked, pointing to my hand.

"My shorties name... Why?"

"Sun... you crazy!!" he said while laughing. "You got it in plain view right on your hand!! Shorty got you sprung and you haven't even smashed her yet," he joked.

On a visit with my mom... she reached over and grabbed my hand to take a look.

"What's that?" Mom asked.

"My girl's name," I answered.

I could see in my mom's face she thought I was going crazy.

"Don't worry... I'ma put your name on me too... maybe on my neck or something."

42

My mom just looked at me then studied my hand again, shaking her head.

About a month later I took some photos and one was a close up where I was holding my chin so you could clearly see the tattoo on my hand. I took a few photos like that to make sure at least 2 were on point. A few days later when I got the photos back, I picked the best one and put it in a card that I had designed especially for Oceasia and I mailed it to her.

About 4 days later as the cell doors were unlocked, I made it downstairs to the ground floor where the computers were. I punched in my digits and went to my emails. I saw that I had numerous emails from Oceasia. As I opened them to read them, I read that she was very overwhelmed and happy about seeing that photo with her name tatted on my hand. She was so happy and wanted me to call her right away. Within an hour we were talking on the phone.

"I got to come and see that tattoo... gotta make sure you ain't faking on me by having a fake tatt for the photo, knowing you didn't get it," she joked.

"You can't be serious Ma. You got me faking on you?" I asked her.

"I was just kidding Bae," she said.

"Nah... you wasn't... you said that because that's something you would do so you only thinking like that cause that's how you would get down," I said.

43

"Really, Bae?... you would think that about me?" she asked, sadly.

"Nah... I was just kidding," I said, mimicking her response.

I laugh now about all of that because when we get in our arguments and love quarrels and I tell her I'm tired of her bullshit, she keeps reminding me that she is a part of me because her name is tatted on me.

There were times when I told her that that's the hand that I hold my iron with when I'm in bed at night thinking about her... or the hand I use to jerk off with thinking about making love to her or to really piss her off I would tell her that the same hand with her name tattooed on it is the same hand I wipe my ass with when I'm taking a dump. That really pisses her off.

"Meet me at the altar in your white dress /

we ain't getting no younger we might as well do it /

been feeling you all the while girl I must confess

Let's get married"

Let's get married

Jagged Edge

Oceasia had been talking about us getting married… that seemed to be the topic every time we spoke on the phone and in her letters. You see I said "her" letters. It wasn't much I could do due to the fact that I was in prison with a long sentence so all I could do was listen and agree. I couldn't destroy or mess up her dreams.

I recall building with this one brother about relationships. He had a life sentence. No… he had several life sentences. He was explaining about never messing up a female's fantasy no matter what. If that is what she wants to talk about… let her talk about it. I'm not saying that I didn't want to marry Oceasia. I just wasn't in the position to push the issue about marriage. I had a 480 months (40 year) sentence, what could I do?

"Listen Oceasia. I love you and all but I got four decades to do and the reality of it is you may not stick around that long. I'm in prison and you're out there." Nah, I wasn't going to do that. I loved her as much as she loved me. I think I had already proven that by still rocking with her and accepting her back with child included. Evher Peace was now in the picture.

Was she serious about getting married? And if she were serious, would I take it there and marry her? She was already using my last name but was she representing me to the fullest to the point that she actually could be Mrs. Edwards? To talk that talk is one thing but to actually walk that walk as well, is showing and proving… and that's a whole other story. Everybody can talk but not many can actually walk that walk… and I had a very long walk… regardless, I'm not the type to just marry whoever's willing to walk that long journey with me. She had to be all of that and then some because even though I was locked up with a stretch to do, I was still "like that" and wasn't settling for just anything. So I wasn't pushing the issue because I wasn't in position to push it. I didn't know how far she would take it so it was all on her.

One day, she took it to that level by smashing the gas so to speak, by writing me a letter of intent to show that she really intended on marrying me, that I meant the world to her and that her love for me was more than eternal. She mailed me a copy of the letter, as well as my counselor, case manager and unit manager. So from there she started filing the paperwork to obtain a marriage license. She started sending me printed copies of wedding rings for me to choose, and was constantly questioning me about which ring I liked the most. I was stuck between the tri-colored gold band and the rose gold wide band. I wasn't allowed to have any wedding bands with stones, so she wanted me to pick a nice one that was temporary while I was incarcerated. I just got my four top gold teeth removed and got my teeth fixed and whitened. Oceasia was really showing me that she was going to make her dreams of being married to me, a reality.

I remember opening the chapter in *Love, Hell or Right* with "Getting Married" by Nas... but not only did Nas marry the love of his life, Kelis, they had a beautiful healthy son and a very ugly divorce just as quick as they had gotten married and all that was always in the back of my mind. Oceasia and I stayed talking on the phones. I called sometimes four to five times a day, sometimes more than that. I was securing other phone lines and burning those 300 minutes crazily. She wanted to know what flavor wedding cake I wanted and everything. I explained to her that I wouldn't get to eat that, but she still kept on. She even made

47

me promise that we were going to have a big wedding once I came home... this was just something for now but she wanted all the glitter and trimmings and everything that came with it once I was on free land.

She started sending me photos of her trying on numerous wedding gowns and different styles and the print out forms for wedding planners. She wrote me and asked me for my list of songs that I wanted to hear at our wedding. I wasn't really taking her serious on that request until one night I called and she brought it up.

"I'm still waiting on your list of songs for our wedding, so you better have it ready by next week."

I was like... "Huh?"

"You heard me... If you can huh, then you can hear... have that list ready!!" she screamed.

So I started making out my list of songs. Then we started getting in little love quarrels. You got to overstand that I'm from NYC and grew up in an era that birthed Hip Hop, so I am kind of old school when it comes to music. I messed with all kinds of music from the 70's to the 90's and some of today's. From the Isley's, Jagged Edge, Jaheim, Janet Jackson, Freddie Jackson, Jodeci, Keith Sweat, Kem, Baby Face, R.Kelly, Shalamar, Dru Hill, Tony, Toni, Tone, After 7, Mint Condition etc... It's way too many to even try to name. My list could be twenty pages or more. We started quarreling about my long lists. We argued about how many songs I could have... from twenty to my top five songs. I was like "five songs?" I argued some more so she submitted and let me get seven songs. Here are my seven songs:

- Make it Last Forever by Keith Sweat & Jacki McGhee

- Let's Chill by Guy

- For the Lover in You by Shalamar

- Let's Get Married by Jagged Edge,

- Calling Your Name by Frederick

- Love of my Life by Brian McKnight

- Am I Dreaming by Atlantic Starr

Believe me when I tell you that narrowing down my list to those specific seven songs, out of so many was very, very difficult so much so, I made her agree to two extra songs because it was on both our lists. "I Want to Thank You" by Alicia Myers and "Spend My Life with You" by Eric Benet featuring Tamia.

She was making all those plans to come to Florida to go to the County Courthouse to get the marriage license. She went and got a copy of my birth certificate and filed for a copy of my social security card after I sent her a notarized letter giving her power of attorney to get them for me. She made plans to move to Florida and stay with my mother who has a nice big house that she is living in by herself. She wanted to be as close to me as possible, while I was still in USP Coleman II in Coleman, Florida.

49

All these plans were on the table while I was putting moves in effect to generate us a little money so we could be semi-alright for a minute. It was at least a good 10 months before all this talking and planning was nothing but talking and planning of plans that kept us fussing and arguing and not getting us anywhere near getting married.

Loyalty Honor and Respect

"Money Goes... Honey Stays"

Fabulous featuring Jay-Z

CHAPTER 6

Your girl is always talking that shit... she don't realize that she is pushing you away with the "you are not here" or "you are so far away" and "I need you right now." I know you heard the same stories from so many dudes on how their girl started going astray somewhere during the course of his bid and it caused him to start seeking companionship elsewhere. Just because we are physically confined doesn't stop us from straying away as well. That other chick could have been laying in the cut waiting on an opportunity to make herself known. Prison is the time when men are the most vulnerable. The reality of the time you have to be away and losing everything sinks in. This starts to really put its pressure down on your mentals... The idea of how you can't fulfill your responsibilities as a man, being the provider, maintainer and protector of the household and she has to hold shit down.

All she wants to do is argue every time you call... she complain about this or that, or she'd throw something in your face that you did in the past and you thought she forgave you for it... huh? She starts slacking in writing or just stop getting at you all together. She is not doing her "wifey" duties and it's showing... always busy when you call, never picking up or whenever you do catch up with her, she wants to argue about shit that isn't important. We get tired of this headache too and that's where the other chick comes in. Just like you women have that other man in the cut that you think we don't know about, we know the signs and symbols when you are straying away. You just don't know our signs and symbols when we are straying... and no, I'm not going to list them for you to identify.

You are slacking in writing letters, sending photos or not visiting. Now we are able to email back and forth unlimited and you slacking on that too. We need someone who will be there, just to listen, to understand or try to understand... someone to care or at least act like they care... The other woman sometimes just starts out as the substitute and it turns into something else because it starts growing. The door opened because you allowed it to. There is no other reason or no one to blame but yourself. If you were there for him, he would not dare go anywhere else. That other chick doesn't have to look better than you. She knows how to make him laugh. She makes time for him. It's the simplest things that win him over. He still loves you and you still have his heart but that other woman is a distraction right now.

There are too many ways to meet or get hooked up with females. Men in prison talk and gossip just as much as women. There are men who hook up their sisters, female cousins, girl's sister, friend or relative with their comrade in prison. Men in prison work out constantly, build up their physical appearance, mental capacity and spiritual beings because with nothing but spare time on our hands, there is nothing to do but improve self and that's what a lot of men in the free world is lacking that most men in prison take advantage of... bettering one's self. B.U.T. this does not apply to all men in prison. In *Love, Hell or Right*, I spoke on the many different categories of men in prison and I spoke on the women who choose to bid with incarcerated men. She has to be built for this. It is not an easy task. Some stand strong, while others fall off. Some get tired and some do truly deserve better than going through this at all, especially if she feels her man is not worth it. It's all about what the relationship is worth to her.

I met all kinds of females from all kinds of angles, but mostly by convicts that I am locked up with. One particular female had a lot of things going for her. She had been married before and was not divorced. I guess she and her husband were separated. She was a 28-year old, curvy, brown-skinned vixen with no children; a child of Jamaican and Cuban parents. She owned a house, had just bought a condo, she had a nice expensive car and a high position at her job, which paid her lovely. We spoke on the phone from time to time and I told her that I had a girl. She told me that she was single but was dating. One time I called and one of her male friends picked up. She and I had beautiful conversations but overall, I loved my girl. This shorty had so much going for her career-wise, and I liked that about her, but she was truly feeling herself too much and running wild. Shorty was about her money too but I felt that dealing with her was not worth losing what I had with Oceasia. Some disagreed with me but I was looking at the overall picture and within six months, shorty faded out of the picture on her own.

She wasn't the only female I met and conversed with but I look at my worth to my girl and her worth to me and I questioned myself... Is it worth it? Is it worth giving up and destroying what I have with Oceasia? Then I ask myself... What do I really have with Oceasia? Is it that special that I can't find it elsewhere with another female? Am I worth it to her? I been through my share of let downs and disappointments. Do I deserve another? Can I do better? And if I feel that way... why do I stay?

All men, who are locked up, go through times when they wonder where they truly stand with their woman. "Is she truly holding me down... Fuck that... Is she messing around on me?"

It's all about how she's handling my affairs and holding me down like she is supposed to be... Is she letting distractions come between us? Distractions can be anything that makes her lose focus. You don't know what she is doing once the phones get cut off for the night and you are locked in your cell. You only know what she tells you or shows you. The relationship is based on faith and loyalty. You need her to be there whether it's mentally, spiritually, financially or not. You just need someone to show that they care about you.

I ended up going to the box "pending investigation," and being in the box you can only utilize the phone for 15 minutes every 30 days and you can't read or answer your emails. So the only way to stay in communication is by writing letters regularly and that one monthly phone call. You can get two hours behind the glass visits, but the visits gotta be made in advance and approved.

After sitting in the box for numerous months, Oceasia wasn't writing me regularly. She got use to the overdosing of everyday emailing and phone calls where writing letters wasn't a major factor anymore, but I kept it moving. I had a Facebook page that was being maintained and monitored by one of my comrades in the outside world. He sent me a print out of all my FB friends so I went through the print out of thumbnail sized photos and names. I was shooting him messages to send to some asking how we knew each other or from where? I was more or less promoting the *Love* novel. A few females were responding and promising to purchase the novel. A few women on FB responded telling me they knew me from my past dealings in numerous states from back in my heyday. Some were congratulating me on the novel and encouraging me to remain focused and to keep my head up.

One female got at me saying that she really felt the novel and she dug me even more after reading it. She knew a great deal about me. After peeping her return address, I saw that she was from Lorain, Ohio, a place I know very well. I was out there 1988-1991 plus my eldest son was born and raised there. After sitting in the box being bored, me and shorty started communicating about relationships. She was just getting out of a marriage with a man she met while he was locked up. She did 11 years with him while he was bidding in prison. She explained to me how she never missed a visit, and did everything that was supposed to be done for a man in prison. Without her, he wasn't financially stable. He didn't have anything until he met her. She was definitely a come up for him all the way around the board. He went home after doing close to 14 years and started cheating with other women, another chick even had a baby for him. She had a very good job and credit score, and dude was destroying her credit and tearing her down.

What can I say? I mean, here I was penning a novel about what we men go through while locked up and what we dream of... a woman who is all about us and here is a female who was all about her man and was riding with him only to be abused and dogged in the end. I said to myself "she must be ugly or she's very difficult to get along with". It had to be something wrong with her for dude to go and do her like that. She held him down for 11 years straight!!! Yet and still, she understood that I had a girl and from reading my novel she knew and understood that I also really loved my girl. She always commented on how I expressed myself so accurately and on point through words and she was really touched by the novel. She knew my son and his mother's family very well. She grew up in the same neighborhood as my son's mom so she was very familiar with them. She used to always see me, I just didn't know who she was. She spoke on the things she saw and things she knew about me. I had a secret admirer that I didn't know about. She kept emphasizing in a lot of her scribes of how much she was about her man and how independent she was. She worked hard and was the overtime queen at her job. She had children that were grown but she was a few years younger than me. I was familiar with her children's father. He was out there when I was in that neighborhood generating money. He wasn't a major factor but I knew who he was.

To pass time, shorty and I wrote regularly, mostly about relationships and the people I knew from the city of Lorain. I had a big name out there in the late 80's and early 90's. and many years later, my son was a football star and everybody knew of him.

One particular day I was sitting around in the cell, waiting for the mailman to come around with the mail. One thing about being in the box… your pen game steps up crazily and you play the door on the weekdays looking for mail. I got a letter from shorty and she sent me a few photos without me asking. I'm not going to sit here and lie like I didn't want to know what she looked like or never wondered what she looked like. I did think about how shorty looked… and finally, I would be able to see why dude kicked her to the curb once he got out and on his feet but before I get to that, her letter was not and I repeat, was not the reason why I was playing the door for mail. I love Oceasia and was still

57

scribing her, not regularly like every day, like we were while I was in the box in *Love, Hell or Right* but I was scribing her enough and was not getting no feedback period. I was trusting to hear something from her. Instead, this next shorty was writing me and it wasn't like she came at me knowing this. She knew well about Oceasia and my love for her from reading the novel. She just didn't know that we were not in touch. She probably was able to figure that out by how much I was writing her once a week on the regular. Anyway, if she knew or didn't know what she was doing, she knew her place and where my heart was at.

As I opened her letter and looked at the photos she sent, I can't front, Shorty was cute. She had her hair all styled up and nails were done. She was posing like she knew that I was checking her out. I'm not sayin' she was on Meagan Goode or Tichina Arnold status but she wasn't ugly at all. She was decent to be in her forties. As I looked at the next photo, I noticed she took this one so I could get a good look at her body. Her ass was PHAT!! She definitely was working with something… I looked at all 3 photos again. Her breath must stink or she must got a vicious body odor for dude to dog her and kick her to the curb. "Something isn't right about shorty" I thought as I stared at her pics. Then I thought of how beautiful my Earth, Oceasia is… especially to me. Everyone says she looks just like Taraji P. Henson and Taraji looks good!!! As I sat on my bunk to read her letter, it started off…

"Now you see what I look like and what I'm working with so you won't be thinking that maybe I'm a booga and that's why dude dumped me. Now, you tell me what you think and do you remember me from back in the day?"

58

I laughed at that. It was funny because she knew I was thinking that she must be ugly. My celly asked me, "What's so funny, God?"

As I passed him the pics to look at, I explained everything to him about shorty from beginning to end, about shorty and why she sent me the three photos and that I was laughing at her comments and the whole situation.

"Yo," as he studied the photos, "Your girl ain't going to dig this. I know she read your novel and know about Tammi and others but to go through it again?" he said laughing.

"Yeah, but look, she is slacking in a lot of areas... we just vibin:" I said in an attempt to justify my giving her so much attention.

"Yeah, but she digs you from way back... she told you that... then to top it off, she orders your novel and feels you even more after liking you twenty years ago? She's going to come between you and your Earth, especially if your Earth is slacking. Shit may turn around and become part 2 of *Love, Hell or Right".* He laughed again.

"I'm not going to let it get that far" I assured him.

"Shorty already feeling you. She knows Oceasia is not playing her part because if so, you and her wouldn't be vibing. Believe me, she knows what she is doing," he proclaimed, handing the pictures back to me. "Best thing to do is dead writing shorty now before she becomes a problem. Matter-fact, pass her off to me. I need her right now" he pleaded.

59

"Nah… I'm not passing her off" I said.

"She is going to be a problem for you and your girl… watch God" he warned.

"I want a chick that look good and cook good /

Cinderella fancy but she still look hood"

Ghetto Dreams

Common featuring Nas

CHAPTER 7

Shorty wrote me a letter asking me what it is that a man looks for in a woman. "What does a man in prison want?" She was still in pain from her dealings with her husband... a dude whom she met while he was in prison doing 14 years. She rode 11 straight years with him, only to get dogged and kicked to the curb for some bum chick. Listening to her story was a sad story in itself. She did everything a man in prison would want and need. She was a seasoned vet when it came to holding her man down. The thing with me was I had a girl and wasn't looking for a side chick but I still continued to correspond with shorty.

I told her to listen to the song "Ghetto Dreams" by Common featuring Nas. It was on Common's "The Dreamer, The Believer" CD track #2. She wrote me telling me about the things she did for dude and how he was well taken care of because she went hard for him. She liked to workout to the point that she worked out at her job. They had a workout room there. She did a lot to keep her ass phat and body tight. She wanted to keep up with the younger chicks, look-wise and body-wise, and all to keep her man happy. I asked her what made her ride with dude and what hurdles did she have to get over. She told me that she was in touch with a friend who was locked up in prison, who she wrote to from time to time. He plugged her into one of his comrades. He knew all the right things to say, how to cheer her up, make her laugh, brighten up her day and one thing led to another. They went from writing each other, playing mail tag to running up the phone bill with the collect calls to her traveling hours of highway driving to come see him every weekend. She fell in love with dude, not knowing that he was a heartless opportunist and he was playing her. She said they had their happy moments too, to the point where she married him. He never even loved her. He told her that when she caught him cheating and he wasn't trying to hide the fact that he was cheating on her. He destroyed her credit and ran up all kinds of bills that she was working overtime to pay. At some point when she and I were keeping in touch, she was working on getting their divorce finalized but of course, he kept standing her up on court dates and putting her through the bullshit.

She wrote me and mentioned how she knew my girl wasn't there for me at the time but she didn't try to disrespect her or nothing. She just said that any woman that got a man who loved her enough to write over 370 something pages about her and his love for her, is something to really die for. That made me really take a minute to soak that all in before I realized that she was absolutely correct. That just opened up the door for us to correspond more through writing letters.

Everything that she did for dude, I didn't need. I was financially good. I had a little over 10 gees in my account and was working on my case. I was still in the box pending investigation. They were recommending transferring me to another Fed Max pen.

I was waking up early in the mornings and getting my workout in, taking a shower and going to the rec yard for my one hour of recreation. This was my daily routine, along with reading, writing, listening to the radio after 4 pm and waiting on the mail. The new Federal drug amendment 750 came into effect

November 1, 2011, so I was on top of that as well as my state ordeal that was run wild to my federal sentence.

One day while on the rec yard, this one white C.O., who acted like he was very racist, was working our range in Special Housing Unit [SHU] aka the "box". USP Coleman 1 and 2 was mostly run by staff, who were either Black or Hispanic. There weren't too many white C.O.'s or administration there so it was crazy to see a C.O. who was racist toward the Black convict population because the C.O.'s superiors who he answered to were Black. But this C.O. was overdoing his job and was a straight up ass hole who was disliked very much by the convicts on USP 1 and 2 compounds. One day he was working our range, telling us to be ready and standing at our door for rec; beds must be made, cells clean and if we go out he is going to shake our cells down for contraband and extra clothes; that right there made most of the range refuse to go to rec. That was one of the tactics he used because he knew we didn't like losing our extra clothes and excessive possessions, I mean, we were already in the box. I still decided that I was going out to rec. I just hid what I wanted real good because my celly was going outside for rec too. After being cuffed, brought out of my cell and led towards the rec yard, I had to be patted down, then "wanded" with a handheld metal detector. I saw the so-called racist C.O. on my way out and he made a remark to me saying, "You are one of those Florida guys who loves the nice weather, huh?" as he was trying to be funny because I chose to come to rec instead of ducking rec like the others.

"What makes you think I'm from Florida?" I asked.

"Hey... I can't tell none of you guys apart. No matter where you from... shit I'm from Ohio," he said.

"Ohio?" I answered, knowing he slid in that racist comment.

"Yeah, the Buckeye state... where their prison system is the worst. You guys will melt in there" he said smiling with his rotten tooth smile.

"Melt?" I laughed. "In Ohio? Stop it. I was in Mansfield back in 1989. Shit was like Jolly Ranchers candy when I was there."

"You was in the Old Castle?" He was shocked to hear that.

"Yeah... R151-291 was my number" I announced as I was led into one of the rec yard cages.

He walked away after standing there looking at me like he was studying me.

After 30 minutes of my workout... Mr. Racist C.O. came back to my cage.

"Edwards," he called as he approached, addressing me by my last name.

"Yeah," I replied.

"I looked you up, you ain't lying, you were in Ohio" he smiled.

From there he started conversing with me everyday, talking about Ohio. He was a C.O. in one of the roughest pens in

Ohio. Made it to Sergeant but the recession came and took over. The budget was cut and a lot of people got laid off, him being one of them so he came to work in the Feds. He said the pay wasn't the same but the benefits were great. We spoke a lot, to the point where he was a push over to me. I made him leave us alone on the range when he worked. He looked up my prision history and saw that I used to be a "terrorist" until I started laying back and grew up. He respected me because he knew I was solid and stood my ground no matter what the odds were, especially in a day and age when most in this generation are just easily broken and quick to tell.

He liked to compare the Ohio state prison to the Feds speaking on how easy we had it in the Feds... that's why he was such an asshole. He was envious of how much power and rights Federal prisoners held and how we were able to file grievances or write up the very same officers who watched over us. He asked me if I was getting out soon, which at first, I wouldn't answer because I knew he already looked me up. I would just ignore the question and keep working out.

One day he asked me about my Ohio sentence, which I knew he already knew about. I told him that it was run wild to my federal sentence because I went to trial on both cases, so they ran it wild. He was explaining to me that the state of Ohio was going through a recession and how it affected the Ohio prison system. He told me that if I get a good lawyer they can get the state time run concurrent with my federal time. I asked him how that was possible. He knew a little bit about Ohio law. He said that he couldn't recommend a lawyer because he wanted to protect himself but he told me to go seek legal advice on that issue. He was 100% sure that it could be done easily.

"All the state of Ohio wants is to give you a number so they can use it in their census to generate money… that's what it's all about Edwards… Money," he spoke so I took that and ran with it.

I got in touch with shorty and explained what I was trying to do. I asked her to get in touch with a good lawyer to see if he could get both sentences run together. She got back at me telling me she spoke to several and one said he needed to read my transcripts to see if it was possible and what angle he could come in to get it done.

Thing was, I was in the box and my property and all my legal paperwork was in storage so I was unable to get to them. I had to try a few moves to get to it, but none worked. I put in several request forms to the SHU property officer to bring me my legal property and that didn't work either. I had an extra set of my trial transcripts at my mother's house so in a letter, I told shorty to hold tight. I would get the transcripts to him and I asked her to send me his office address and price he would charge for a consultation. She wrote me back a week later, telling me that she went to the courthouse and paid for my trial transcripts and had them delivered to the attorney. She already paid the fee for him to review them. I was kind of shocked because I didn't ask her to do that, nor did I need her to do it, so I expressed that in my response to her. She wrote back, stating that she was definitely feeling me like that so she was willing to do whatever it took to get me home, even if it wouldn't bring me home to her.

I respected that, but I felt some way about it because I'm not with taking advantage of a woman. She had a beautiful heart and spirit. I wrote her telling her that I'm not the type to take advantage of her beautiful heart. That's what dude did. He saw how she was willing to go all out and he abused her. I, on the other hand, wasn't like that.

I saw her outside beauty and inner beauty. I told her to tell me how much the fee cost so I could repay her but she refused. I wrote her, thanking her for her kindness and all and told her she was a beauty. She hit me back saying she was feeling that name so much that it was going on her license plate. So I guess her new name was … "Beauty."

"Bad Habits"

Maxwell

CHAPTER 8

An old head from Washington, D.C. who had been locked up for the past 25 years, read *Love, Hell or Right* while he was in the SHU. He told me one day that "that girl of yours Oceasia got her hooks in you." I laughed it off but I knew it was true because I loved that girl and never even slept with her or anything.

A C.O. came to my door and told me that he was reading the novel. I was getting letters from heads in prison, who forwarded letters to the publishing company telling me how they felt the novel. I heard from everyone, except Oceasia. I even sent her an autographed copy so I knew she had it and eventually read it. By now, I thought I would have heard from her, at least voicing her angry thoughts and speaking on certain things in the novel or possibly expressing happiness based on me producing the very first "God and Earth Love Novel" ever to go to print, in which, I expressed my feelings to her and for her. I made them public by putting them in a novel... only to not hear from her about my first published book at all.

Me and my side-piece I called shorty, who was now known as "Beauty", were keeping in touch. For the most part, she talked about her job, doing overtime on her job and working out.

I was in tune with my street team and comrades as well as corresponding with a few females along the way. I'm a street General who's been locked up since 1993. I know how to move and how to make moves that count.

I went to sign up for the law library, which at that time, was computerized. I had to log in with my nine-pac digit number after inputting my registered number and four-digit pin. The only option that I was able to utilize was the one with the law library section but I was able to see that within the last 31 days, I had over 116 unread emails. I wasn't allowed to go in my emails to read them or even see who they came from. I knew Oceasia was getting at me because she was emailing me like 10 times a day when I was in population. Ever since Coleman got the email access, Oceasia had been using that instead of physically writing letters.

The Federal Bureau of Prison system had us utilizing emails and was giving us access to MP3's to buy and download censored music, but I was in the box so I couldn't enjoy any of those privileges, I had to be in population to do so. By now, I had Beauty's house number, cell phone number and email address. I knew a great deal about her and her life. She was connecting me to a lot of people that I knew in her city of Lorain and reconnecting the ones I had lost contact with over the years. Mostly everything she was doing for me was on the strength of her knowing me years ago, having great respect for me and her overstanding the struggles of a man in prison, after all, she rode with a fake dude for eleven years.

"Beauty" was taking the double-sided fliers of my novel and putting them up in hair salons and barbershops all around her city. She was setting up webpages to post my ads. She was helping to push me and my Earth's love story, she even took a photo of her holding up the novel to post on her FB page. She was doing all this on the strength. She was even communicating with my street team and helping out.

71

It takes a certain type of woman to deal with a man in prison. I was listening to a radio show where the host was speaking about watching a reality show that highlighted women who had relationships with men in prison. He spoke on the hardships women go through and was amazed at how love alone, can push these women to be these men's backbones. In return, his co-host, who was a female, was talking down on women who deal with men in prison. She said that those women must have very low self-esteem or they are not capable of attracting or holding onto a man in the free world so they deal with men in prison.

She spoke on how they must be "society's rejected" or out of shape, fat women. She hammered that those are the type of women that men in prison target and abuse. She couldn't believe that there were websites and pen pal services that catered to men in prison. These are companies that cater to the prison population. She claimed that a female must be out of her mind to even go through anything with a man who is in prison. She talked bad about us men. They even had callers calling in with their stories and input. Every caller had a unique story to tell. Just about all of them were women, some with very high IQ's, some with very good paying jobs and high positions. Some callers claimed to be far from out of shape or fat and more than enough were claiming to be straight up beautiful.

Some of the women calling in to the radio show, knew the men before they went to prison and some met the men while they were in prison. Their relationships were special to them. Most spoke on what attracted them to men who are locked up. First up was the kind of men that were in the free world, what they had to choose from and work with. Today's men are lazy, and not motivated to become leaders and providers. Some want to be womanizers with multiple women and a lot of them are gay or bisexual. There are a few good men in the batch of today's society of men. Most of the real men are locked up in prisons. Prisons are filled with men. There are more Black men in prison than in college and there are more Black men locked up, than were in slavery in the 1800's. Women can't find a good Black man or a good man, period, because we are being warehoused in prison.

In the United States alone, there are close to 3 million people who are incarcerated. In the Federal Prison System, there are over 217,000 inmates, which includes prisoners sentenced under D.C.'s criminal code. In my home state of New York, the prison population is over 58,000. These statistics come out of an almanac of facts. Prison is a multi-billion dollar business. A lot of companies generate their money from prisons from building them, warehousing prisoners or just doing business with state, Federal or private prisons.

We men are human beings, we have families too so why shouldn't a woman love us? The most beautiful thing about a woman, who stands by her man in prison, is her heart. She has a beautiful heart and that is what counts. People want to talk bad about us men in prison but even though prison is a very fucked up place, it can and will change the way a man thinks and lives... for better or worse.

In religions, most of God's prophets and messengers were the lowly of men and had been in prison before. Some of the greatest men of our times and of our history were in prison. From

73

Nelson Mandela, Malcolm X and a great many others. A diamond must go through extreme heat and extreme pressure to become a diamond. Some men come to prison and use it as a learning center and learning experience by learning a trade, several languages and the stock market. Some earn their G.E.D. and college degrees in prison. Everybody that goes to prison isn't a bad or awful person. They just made a mistake or mistakes in life and had to pay for it. We are still human.

I salute all women, who stand by their men, for having the heart to face this struggle we go through behind these enemy lines. I tip my hat to women who overstand this shit and still accept us despite our downfalls.

Whenever Oceasia and I used to go through our little quarrels or big arguments and she threw that "You're in prison" shit in my face or started talkin' that "I'm tired of being here." I always reminded her... "If it wasn't for me being in prison, we would have never met. Everything happens for a reason. If I didn't go through what I'm going through now, you and I would never have crossed paths. We are together because of this bid and where I was at that particular time when I picked up the Five Percenter Newspaper and read your article back in 1999. If I was in the free world, I would have never written you to commend you on your courage and strength." This bid made me appreciate not only Oceasia, but ALL women so when she talks that shit, I remind her what brought us together and if she leaves me now... she's going to leave me in the same place she met me... PRISON...

"I can love you better than she can"

I Can Love You

Mary J. Blige featuring Lil Kim

CHAPTER 9

They say once a good girl goes bad, she is gone forever. But what about when a bad guy goes good? A lot of females are attracted to the bad guys... that's what got them going at men in prison. But not all those bad guys are the bad guys they claim to be... some just made a bad choice and got caught up... either way, they are labeled as "Bad Guys."

I didn't know what "Beauty" saw in me or what she was attracted to for her to be feeling me. She was an independent, hard working female with a very good heart. She was charming, had a tight body and could probably get any man she wanted. She knew that I was deeply involved with a woman and She understood how prison relationships go and the struggles that came with it. I had to ask her something... "Why are you on me like this?" She responded by saying that back in the day when I was out there (In Ohio), I was spoken about by just about every female she knew. Then one day she got to actually see me and she liked what she saw. But that was then... years had gone by and our lives went in the directions they did. Twenty-three years later, she saw my photo on someone's page she befriended on Facebook so she put in a Facebook request to my page. Yes, I have a Facebook page even though I've been locked up so long, I had somebody maintaining my page and they accepted Beauty's friend request. Beauty said it wasn't until she read my novel that she got to know how I thought and felt about love. It was the way I expressed the meaning of love. The words I used. The way I bore my soul and true feelings. All these things "made her melt". She understood where I was coming from in that sense because that's how she felt when she was dealing with dude she bid with for eleven years. She saw dude and Oceasia in the same lime light, cut from the same cloth and felt that they didn't appreciate true love. She said that her thoughts were something that she felt and were not intended to cause confusion between me and my girl. She was not trying to do that. It was just that I asked and she felt she could be open about it. She knew that I was not going to leave Oceasia for her. She didn't expect that and she respected Oceasia as a woman. She read the novel and knew that I loved Oceasia deeply. She understood how Tammi felt. She explained that my explanation to Tammi as to why I chose to remain in a relationship with Oceasia instead of being with her, was something that made her cry. It was so beautiful.

She said that it was when she finished reading the novel that she felt what she felt and also that she could love me better than Oceasia ever could. Not a physical love either. It starts out mentally and spiritually. She loved my mind and wanted us to really get to know each other well before taking the friendship to the physical love level. She said that I deserved to be loved back just as hard as I was loving Oceasia. She was not trying to pull me away from Oceasia or get in Oceasia's way. She just wanted to keep in touch and be real about things. She was thankful for our friendship and what we had going on as far as writing.

It was a very sincere letter and I was still tripping about Beauty's boldness. My celly listened and I told him about the situation and read him the letter. When you have a celly, y'all converse on certain levels, share advice and ideas but only if y'all have certain things in common. My celly in Coleman was cool, he read my novel and was familiar with my situation so once I told him about Beauty, he had this to say…

"I told you she was going to ease her way in!!! Females got vicious game just like we do!!! Now look… she read your novel, y'all started vibing, she knows that you and your Earth are not rocking like that. She knows your Earth's history, how she has a pattern of disappearing for periods of time so she uses your girl's habit of not holding you down all the way, as her way to get in good with you. You see? She already did little things for you. She is helping with pushing YOUR novel about YOUR girl. Now that's some G shit. Then she takes it on her own to get your transcripts and get them to a lawyer. She is trying to involve herself with your war for freedom too? She is showing you that she can hold you down and she is what you need in your corner. You need to dead her and pass her to me!!!" … He smiled but I know that he was dead ass serious.

Beauty is what a prison dude needs in his corner but like I said, I'm not a prison dude. I'm just a dude in prison. I didn't need to take advantage of her kindness and I wouldn't play those games even if I did. I loved Oceasia… so I started falling back some from scribing Beauty.

After that letter, Beauty went back to being the hard worker, who was finding time to post my novel ads up on websites. She was taking my fliers and leaving them in malls, bookstores, salons and barbershops. Her letters consisted of the moves she made with the fliers and how hard she worked at her job and how she was looking forward to doing overtime. She loved working and getting her money. She didn't speak on her feelings for me anymore. I guess if I didn't touch on it, she wasn't going to go any further with speaking on her feelings. She started inquiring about the Nation of Gods and Earths, about my culture, what I stood for and what it's meaning was. She wanted to understand it more and understand the science of mathematics and the language so she could get a better understanding of the novel. She was lost in the "God body" talk and all the building (verbally demonstrating knowledge between Five Percenters) in the ciphers (man-made circles, in which Fiver Percenters build). She wanted to know what it really meant and to hear it from me instead of going online and getting a misinterpretation. Shorty wanted to know how the women fit in. What role do they play and why there wasn't a lot of Earths around that she would have at least seen one to be familiarized with, knowing how to spot one. She wanted to know if there were any Earths in Lorain, Ohio? Maybe Cleveland? If so, where were they in Ohio? She asked a lot of questions. I guess that was her way of keeping me near her because I'm always and forever going to show and prove. I made it where that was the subject that we were going to stick with from that point on and it was going good. Until she asked me another question… she wanted to know the difference between her and Oceasia because from where she stood, how saw things, she couldn't tell the difference.

"She said… you ain't no good

but you feel so good

She said… I know you bad

but I want you bad."

Leave You Alone

Young Jeezy featuring Ne-Yo

CHAPTER 10

Even with Beauty knowing that I was Oceasia's man and she was trespassing on personal property, she still was at me. She said she just couldn't leave me alone. Shit sounded like Young Jeezy and Ne-Yo's song. I wasn't pushing the issue, it was a known actual fact that I loved Oceasia, but the thing with Beauty was, she was persistent and consistent and very smooth with it. If I went a week or two without scribing her, she would write me thanking me for our friendship and letting her know me. She would tell me how she appreciated that short period of time reading my words. She said she knew that Oceasia would come to her senses and come get what was hers but she questioned me at the end asking... was I totally Oceasia's...

I still hadn't heard from my Earth. What I decided to do was let her find her way back on her own, and until then I was going to do me and vibe with Beauty. What I mean by vibing is just flow back and forth, talking shit. I wasn't leading her on or giving her hints that I was willing to test the waters with her. I had been in the box for ten months, four of them was me and Beauty flowing back and forth. I repeat, for ten moons that I hadn't heard from Oceasia and I had been writing and reaching out to her. So I decided to just do me and have fun.

One thing I didn't like about Oceasia was she was never ever there when I really needed her. She dropped the ball too many times when I needed her to come through. I'm not with the let downs and disappointments and it seemed like that's all that was happening. She didn't allow me to be me nor did she follow my lead. I needed things done to manifest results and nothing ever pulled through when I had to rely on her or her input.

Beauty was showing me otherwise and I wasn't looking for her to do anything. It wasn't her duty to. She had no obligation to me or my cause. I didn't need a female to take care of me. I knew how to make moves. I'm a hard worker and true hustler.

Once upon a time, before I got locked up on my Fed case, I was messing with this female who was real cool. She was a stripper with a bangin' body and a very pretty face. We were doing our thing but I never forgot how we met or what she did for a living. I respected her for being about her business and money plus she was very intelligent and was saving up her cash and making moves but she was still out there.

When I got locked up, blew trial and got sentenced, she still was getting at me. By then, she was featured in "Black Tail" men's magazine, which was a magazine that featured women who posed naked and in soft porn sexual acts. She also was doing light porn movies. She was doing what she had to do to survive. When I was sentenced, she asked if I would marry her. I told her that she must be crazy because I view love and marriage in a whole different light than most people do. I look at it as a life commitment. I told her how she was moving out there didn't coincide with me and my values when it came to love and marraige. She was showing her body and performing sexual acts... couldn't have her coming to see me, wanting to hug and kiss me knowing that she had "meat" in her mouth... Nah... but she said no matter what female I dealt with I still wouldn't know what they were doing, while I'm locked away. She continued to say least I'd know what she is doing and no matter what, I'ma have her to hold me down, riding with me and taking care of me. I told her I still couldn't rock like that.

I had a few women who offered to take care of me. I refused because I didn't need a woman for that. I'm not about taking advantage of women or using them for their money. I need a woman for companionship purposes, where we do for each other. I want her to be there because she wants to be there. I want her to want me as much as I want her. I want to love her and need her just as much as she loves and needs me. I need her to be there at all times like I'll be. Oceasia wasn't there... and it got to the point where not only did I notice but everyone around me noticed too. I don't like to speak on any of her flaws or shortcomings because I really love her but she was really slacking and there was someone who was trying to take her place. I was in a situation where not too many women were going to keep coming into my life, willing to love me for me...

I kept giving Oceasia all these chances and I wasn't feeling appreciated in the end at all. I'm a man who is very big on morals and principles. So loyalty, honor and respect mean a lot to me, even if it does not mean anything to others. I still stand tall on those principles today.

I'm not one of those bum ass dudes or lames who is inconsiderate or unappreciative. I show my appreciation for my

83

Earth as much as possible. Even behind all this concrete, steel and doing hard time, I still make moves and show love to my loved ones.

Coleman 2 has a leather hobby craft shop where convicts can order limited amounts of leather of all kinds and colors. Some of these convicts are very skillful, crafty and creative. I got all kinds of handbags, purses, big bags, knap sacks and just about anything you could imagine, made for Oceasia and other loved ones. Leather, suede, some real ill shit and it wasn't cheap either. Them dudes charged for their work.

I had some skillful artists do custom cards of all kinds from sexual to pop up cards. I did the stuffed pillows, stuffed animals, knitted sweaters and I ordered different colored, flavored chocolate roses and chocolate dicks for her on Valentine's Day too. I write the illest poems that come from my heart. Man listen, I showered Oceasia with all kinds of things. Just seeing all that, one would be surprised to find out I was in prison.

I recall one time I got a black leather handbag made for a female friend who grew up with me. I had it made and sent to her on the strength of us knowing each other for so long. She is kinda like family to my family and I call her maybe every now and then, meaning once every four months or so. I sent her a birthday card. When we spoke and she thanked me, I told her that I had something coming over there for her. Maybe about a month or so later, I called her and we were kicking it about her job, family life and what not. I asked her did she get the present I sent her. She said no. I was surprised that it didn't get there knowing that it was sent over 5 weeks prior. I told her that I would call her back. I went and hollered at my dude who made my bags for me. He has to send the finished work to his people, who in turn, mail them out to your peoples. Convicts always have to find ways to circumvent shit because these devils don't be wanting us to do anything. Selling the handbags is a violation of their policy and bullshit rules. Anyway, I found dude in his usual spot... the leather hobby craft room at inside recreation. Once I explained the situation, he assured me that his peoples had sent the bag out. On a piece of paper that he kept in his custom-made wallet, he even had the date the bag was mailed, the destination and the estimated time it should have arrived. I had to wait another hour before I could head back to the unit to get back on the phone so I ordered another handbag. This time it was for my Earth's niece.

As I made it back and called, I had to ask shorty if she was sure no package came there and I told her the date.

"Nah, Sha... ain't nothing come... What was it anyway?" she asked.

"It was a surprise," I told her.

"Well, the surprise didn't show" she said and we laughed.

I told her that it was a black leather handbag that this cat made just for her. She started screaming.

"Damn, what's up, Ma?" I asked.

"You won't believe this shit, my man handed me a bag just like the one you described. I can't believe he did that shit!!"

I laughed at that shit because it was foul but it was funny too.

"Damn... Someone in prison made that bag? That shit was nice... my girlfriends at work asked me where I got it from... wow"

That's how I rock. I do what I can for my family and loved ones, even if it's sending them some money from my account. I strive to show love and I've been locked up since 1993. How many men in prison do you know do stuff like that? Usually men in prison ask people on the outside for money or for help. I don't get points for that? When my Earth tells me she needs currency, I ask her "how much?" and I send it to her. I pay for traveling fees when she visits. Both dudes who made leather bags for me told me that they made thousands of dollars off of me alone as I blessed my Earth, Evher, my mom, family, and numerous female friends with knapsacks for their children just to put a smile on their faces and show my appreciation. Some cats close to me in prison like to laugh and joke with me that I'm in prison and still "tricking."

"Yeah, call it what you want but I bet your girl wish you got down like I do" I'd joke.

Once a female fucks with me, she just can't leave me alone but being in my position and situation... How many women are willing to fuck with a man like me, who is in prison?

Loyalty Honor and Respect

"Hate me Now"

Nas featuring Puff Daddy

CHAPTER 11

My celly was twelve years younger than me and was very, very competitive. No matter what it was, he wanted to compete and prove that he was better and always ended up losing. He was originally from Pittsburgh but he was getting money in Erie, PA. He was doing his thing but thought he was the smartest, smoothest and illest cat who ever put it down, not knowing and understanding that we all thought like that. In reality, son was slow compared to how I moved. He challenged me in everything… working out, who was getting more money, who had been in more states… the average shit dudes talk and brag about in prison. He spoke on how he was doing it and how he was living. He had flocks of females, luxury cars, plenty money and owned some real estate.

He had been locked up for six years of a ten-year bid for a drug conspiracy. Out of ten years, you can do eight years, ten months. In his six years, he spent up all of his savings trying to ball outta control in prison. He had been in three different institutions and most of his chicks had rolled out on him. His main chick sold his property and ran off with the money. He had less than three years left and was still talking about going home and getting that money. He spoke like the world didn't evolve or change when in reality, nothing was the same, not even the blocks he left but he didn't want to hear that shit.

He kept me laughing overall. He said I was washed up but he kept trying to get as much game out of me as possible. He loved the way I moved.

He was in the "Box" pending an investigation. The administration did a sweep on the compound of all the known move makers. During that process, he got caught up in the sweep "just because..." but you couldn't tell him that. He would argue you down that he was in the middle of it all but when it was time to show and prove, he had a story for that too.

He called himself "Ikey Raw" but everyone called him "Ike." Nevertheless, he was a good dude... he was also a good celly. Even after all his women problems and problems with all three of his children's mothers, he still talked that shit like he was God's gift to women. His motto was, "If a female don't like me... she must be gay!!" He was a wisdom seed [Brown-skinned], medium build, about 5'11" with curly, wavy hair that he kept low and constantly brushed. He stayed in the mirror brushing his hair and as I'm writing this, that's what he's doing... talking that shit.

"Yo, ShaKim Bio. I'm telling you, Ack... I'm on these pen pal websites, "Friends Behind the Wall" and "Write a Prisoner.com"... I'ma come up... my introduction got to be some real playa shit!!! Watch how many shorties get at me, Ack!!" He was at it already.

"Yeah... I hear you. Stop calling me Ack... that ain't my name." I would tell him that all the time.

"Stop it... you know that's a habit I got, Ack. I mean God but yo I'ma plug you with a few old heads if you want 'em. I need young ones. Yo, what's up with shorty from Ohio?"

"Why you keep asking about her?" I asked him on top of his question.

"Because she is already ready... She is the type to ride with her dude. You got that N.O. chick so you should pass shorty off to me" he said.

"I thought you need young ones and not old heads" I reminded him.

He looked at me and started laughing.

"She is a valuable old head and still look like somethin'... you know? See if she got any sisters or crazy friends, cousins or something for Ikey Raw!!" He spoke about himself in the third person as he went back to the mirror, brushing his waves.

"I'm Leaving… On The Next Plane!!!"

My case manager made her weekly rounds on Saturday, early in the morning. She was a real light stepper too so you had to be on extra point to catch her once she came up on your range. She didn't let no one know as she walked through hoping no one stopped her... once she passed your cell she wasn't back tracking so if you missed her, you had to catch her the following week... she was slick like that.

USP Coleman 1 and 2 had mostly Black and Hispanic administration and staff and whenever you got them running an institution, I hate to say it but you could expect laziness and a whole lot of bullshit when comparing it to an institution that's run by White administration and White staff. You can even talk to staff like hood heads.

I'm always up early in the morning... so I heard as Ms. G come up on the range and quietly walked through. As soon as she came to my cell, I popped up to the door's window... "Ms. G. Good morning Ma... What's good?"

"Edwards... I see you up... You don't miss nothin'... huh?"

She stared at me.

Ms. G was very light skinned and on the heavy side... maybe like twenty years ago she was stunning and a head turner. She still had a phat ass on her though. She was about 5'4", wearing tight pants but other than that she was washed up.

"What's my status?" I inquired.

As she looked at her roster with all inmates in her case file, who were housed in the Shu... She found my name and read it.

"They just finished and closed your investigation on Thursday... I am putting your packet together for a transfer."

"Yeah? I'm getting' shipped?" I acted surprised.

"Yeah... They want you outta their pen and want you to be someone else's problem. You did your thing here and been getting away for too long... So take your show on the road" she said as she smiled.

"You doing my transfer packet... So where do you recommend they send me?" I asked.

"I can't tell you exactly where you're going... but it will be within two weeks and it's a plane ride."

"Word?"

"I will tell you this much... the person who keeps calling up here inquiring about you will be real happy if anything," she stated as she flashed her pearly white teeth and walked away from my door with her soft shoes and light steps.

"Ms. G is on the tier y'all... Tryna creep!!" someone yelled, blowing her up.

She quickened up her walk to the front grill to get off the range. I started laughing because she had a job but she didn't like doing it... she was cool though. She gave me a hint that I was headed to California.

"Yo. I heard that God... you out of here," said my celly. Dude was crazy nosey.

93

"Yeah... I'ma be gone on the next bus," I replied.

"No doubt... but you going on a plane... Who you think is calling up here asking about you?" he asked.

"Yo, you need to get someone to call and ask about you instead of worrying about who is worrying about me," I snapped.

"There you go on that bullshit" sighed Ike.

*　*　*

Ten days hadn't passed since I got that news from my case manager that I was being transferred and I was actually packing out. Right after they served breakfast and began the rec pull, a C.O. came to my door.

"Edwards."

"Yeah... What's good?"

"Pack all your shit... R&D is coming to get you within twenty minutes or so... be ready."

"Say no more" I replied.

I took a shower and got ready. I left my celly all my hygiene products and food items. It's really rough in the box and I know how it goes. I packed up all my letters, photos, my address book, legal papers and so on and hollered down the range at a few of my closest comrades. I left my watch with my celly with instructions to pass it on to one of my dudes. I told him to stay focused and always on point, then I dapped him up with a pound and brotherly embrace.

"I'm gone, Ike."

"Hold shit down ShaKim Bio... stay a 'G,'" he responded.

"No doubt." I said

*　　*　　*

Several C.O.'s came up on the range and came to my cell door.

"Edwards... let's ride."

As I was handcuffed through the slot in the door, they also handcuffed my celly before opening the cell, escorting me out and off the range. You could hear convicts all over the Shu on the six ranges hollering and shouting. A few were calling out my name wishing me luck and farewells. There were two other convicts who were leaving as well. As we were walked through the maze of doors towards R&D, where we were stripped naked and searched, given dark blue paper pants and paper shirts and the Kung Fu blue slide sneakers to dress in.

My property was already there, being packed. They took the property I had under my arm and packed it with the rest of my property.

"Have any dentures, partial plates, wedding bands, or glasses?" I was asked.

"No" I responded. As I was re-cuffed and put in leg shackles and a chain going around my waist with my cuffs went through an iron loop on the belly chain.

I was put on a fake looking Greyhound bus with tinted windows. The bus had about 15 other convicts from Coleman's complex. The Coleman complex was the largest federal complex in the U.S. It had pen 1, pen 2, a men's FCI, a men's low and a women's camp. Altogether, it housed over 5,000 inmates. As the bus made its way to the FCI to pick up more convicts, there were 4 mini-vans following for extra security. A couple of female inmates were in the vans and there were about six unmarked vehicles with C.O.'s and U .S. Marshals armed with heavy artillery to make sure the goods were delivered without incident.

Usually, we were taken to USP Atlanta to the holdover, from there we were housed and shipped by either plane or bus to different federal institutions.

USP Atlanta was where we were received, sort out, packaged and sent out like merchandise. USP Atlanta was also where a lot of the good-looking female C.O.'s were. So many convicts, like myself, didn't mind going through that spot even though the food and living conditions were terrible but bearable if you were coming from or going to a white staffed, white administration run institution. So, we valued spots like USP Atlanta.

96

CHAPTER 12

The bus wasn't going to USP Atlanta. We took all kinds of back roads and highways to main streets then back roads to highways.

I had a window seat so I was looking at the cars and license plates as well as the road signs. We were headed to Tampa. Once we got to Tampa, we kept on going to Jacksonville, which was still headed north towards Georgia, but with all these government cars and vans in route with us, I knew better.

After about two hours or more on the road, we pulled off the highway and took a lot of back roads to a backyard military base. The Feds usually used military bases by the Army or some armed forces base for their pick-ups and drop offs with their federal airlines.

The U.S. Marshals have planes to ship convicts all over the U.S. We pulled in onto the military base and drove nonstop to who knows where. After about twenty minutes, we came to a stop where there were thirty-some buses and vans with several prison and jail deputies posted up with shotguns and automatic weapons of all calibers. We sat on the bus for about another hour before the buses and vans moved again. All the vehicles were lined up towards the runway as all the C.O.'s and Marshalls came out and stood with weapons. You could see the approaching aircraft coming... looking like a 747 or some shit as it landed and drove towards us.

Once it came to a stop and opened up, Marshalls came down the portable steps and got in position, surrounding the plane with weapons as a gas tanker came and refueled the plane.

We saw convicts, males and females, come off the plane. They were checked and lined up in various lines outside waiting to get on one of the lined up buses or vans. As U.S. Marshalls approached the buses, they were calling convicts off and lining them up for receiving purposes of the awaiting aircraft. This went on for another thirty minutes or so before the bus I was on was next. A Marshall came on board and shouted

"When you hear your name, come to the front and give me your register number as you step off the bus!"

He started calling out names. About ten names later, my name was called.

"Edwards... John Edwards."

I rose up and walked towards the front and spit my register number out

"26499 - 083."

I stepped down off the bus and was directed to an awaiting Marshall, who checked my cuffs and leg shackles. He then asked me to open my mouth and stick out my tongue, then he pat me down and directed me to another line that was waiting to load on the plane.

Shit is crazy how we get shipped all over the U.S. to different fed and private owned prisons. This shit is a multi-billion dollar business... true slavery... warehousing convicts I thought to myself as we all stared and quietly lusted over the female prisoners who were lusting and staring right back at us as they tried to impress us with their phat asses and good... and bad looks.

Convicts looked across at others in different lines, some acknowleding those they knew or were familiar with, while others were mean mugging just because. I saw a few dudes I knew but we couldn't really hold conversations... just head nods.

"Yo, Peace God!" one convict I knew hollered.

"What's good?" I asked.

"Where to?" he asked.

"Out west" I said as he shook his head at me.

"Where you going?" I asked.

"Lee County" he responded.

"Ok, tell Green Eye Preme that ShaKim Bio said what's up." I told him as the police told him to shut up and he fell in line for the awaiting bus.

At that moment I was being directed up the steps to the plane.

The plane had reached its capacity, filled with convicts of every color and nationality. Females were seated in the front of the plane. As I was lead past them to the middle of the plane and

99

given a window seat where I was "black- boxed" in. "Black-boxed" is when a black box is put over the chain part of your handcuffs so you can't move your wrists. I've had max custody status since 2000 and ever since then, I've gotten the "black-box" treatment.

I looked around and everyone was seated and holding conversations. These conversations amongst convicts were about any and everything from sports, law, gossip or prison-to-prison news. Thirty minutes later, as I started looking out the window, we were racing down the runway and in the air, flying the friendly skies.

*　　*　　*

I was glad to finally get off that plane, after being cuffed and shackled, with a black box on top of that, for several hours as we flew over numerous states landing to drop some off and pick even more up plus, they fed us peanut butter and jelly sandwiches, dry ass pretzels and a bottle of water, all which are extremely hard to consume while you're "black-boxed". I was glad when we landed at the Federal Transfer Center in Oklahoma.

The Federal Transfer Center is where convicts, male and female, get processed all day, everyday, even illegal immigrants being deported go through the Transfer Center. I went through the hours of being processed in and being evaluated before being changed into khaki brown pants and a brand new white t-shirt and boxers. Because I am max custody, I was sent to the box on the 7th floor with no celly. The food there was cool and we got rec Mon-Fri for 1 hour.

I stayed for two days then I was woken up at 4 am and I went through the process of being geared up to eat, get dressed, I was cuffed, shackled and "black-boxed" again and put on another plane. That was another two and a half hour process. Then it was back to flying and making two or three more stops before heading out west to California.

I was dead tired when we landed in California. I was called off the plane with about thirty-five other convicts and we were put on another bus that took us to USP Victorville, which was ten minutes away from where we landed.

USP Victorville Complex was in Adelanto, California, which was in the southern part of Cali and about two and a half hours away from Los Angeles so during that time, I was literally so close to Oceasia and she didn't even know it.

Victorville had a penitentiary, two mediums and a female camp. As the bus pulled into the prison complex, they first went to the mediums to drop off convicts before heading over to the pen. As we drove for another fifteen minutes and were able to see the tall gun towers come into sight, we knew we were approaching USP Victorville. It was built exactly like the Coleman pens.

When I got locked up in 1993, there were only 5 Federal penitentiaries and 1 supermax in the United States. They were USP Lewisburg in Pennsylvania, USP Atlanta in Georgia, USP Terre Haute in Indiana, USP Leavenworth in Kansas and USP Lompoc in Cali. The super-max was in Illinois, called USP Marion.

In 1995, when I came into the federal system, they had just opened up USP Allenwood in Pennsylvania, USP Florence in

Colorado and the super, super-max ADX, also in Florence, Colorado. In 1998, USP Beaumont opened in Texas. By this time, there were over seventeen U.S. Federal Penitentiaries across the United States. They went from five to eight to seventeen pens. Most of the five original pens turned into mediums, except USP Lewisburg, which is a Special Management Unit [SMU] used as a disciplinary spot for convicts who stay in trouble and can't adjust to the so called rules.

Prison was a booming business as they kept buiding more prisons to hold more and more people. I was being housed at USP Victorville on 'hold over status,' meaning I, along with others, was being housed there until the next bus rode out to northern California to the other USP... USP Atwater. That was another six to eight hour ride so I felt let down, knowing I was being shipped even further into California. Being so close to Oceasia quickly left my mind as I was processed for temporary containment over in USP Victorville's holdover unit.

The holdover unit was equipped to hold one hundred and fifty convicts per unit and there were two units. Altogether, USP Victorville had six buildings cut in half. There were two sides, making it a total of twelve units. One building was being used as the holdover unit and it was on the compound. We were able to look out the window into the general population as they went back and forth during rec moves, on the yard and during chow. They were on the move and weren't allowed to stop at the window. C.O's stood there to make sure that they kept it moving accordingly. The holdover unit was built and run just like a regular unit. We were let out of the cell for three hours a day, to utilize phones, emails, and showers. The food there was ok, it was brought to the unit and passed out by C.O.'s and orderlies.

It mattered what side you were on to look out the window onto the compound. I was on the side where I could look out my cell's window and see everything. A few N.Y. convicts came over to holler at me, as well as a few convicts I knew such as Jesse Cage. He was an old head and big name out of New Orleans. Dr. Mutulu Shakur, who was Tupac's father and mentor, was also there.

There were several convicts that I was familiar with in the unit, who were also in route to USP Atwater. My manz, Amir from PA, who is also an author... my manz Star from Queens, who is part of the Lost Boyz family. I was told that I just missed Qasim from Hollis, who I knew from the streets. Qasim discovered D.J. Irv later know as Irv Gotti.

For some reason, my phone was off and it took me four days to get it turned on. I went through a lot to get it fixed but in the meantime, I did get to utilize the computer where I had ten months worth of emails.

Oceasia was emailing crazily in the early months. I read as many emails as I could before moving on to the showers and other things.

I put Beauty's email on my request list, which she approved that same day and we began emailing each other back and forth almost immediately. I only had three hours and believe me, time moved fast and waited for no one. Beauty wanted me to call her so bad just so she could finally hear my voice. I told her through the email that I would call whenever I was able.

The first person I called was my mother to put her on point as to me being shipped to Cali and to let her know that I was ok.

"Son... wha gwaan? I'm glad you call," she said in her heavy Jamaican accent.

"Hi Mom... I'm ok... They shipped me way out here to California."

"What??... California!!... that's unbelievable... I just came to see you not even two weeks ago," she chatted.

"Yeah, Mom... I know."

"That's messed up... that messed up your surprise" she said.

"What you talking about, Mom?"

"Hold on... someone wants to speak with you. Hold on a minute."

"Peace Bae!!!"

I couldn't believe whose voice I was hearing.

"Hello?" I said with a big question mark over my head.

"Oh, that's how you address your wife? What? You not happy to hear from me?" she said.

Shit was un-fucking believable... Oceasia was at my mom's house in Florida and was coming to see me that weekend. I had to call back when the phone beeped. She told me that she wrote me and sent me letters, telling me that she was coming to Florida to see me... she and Evher.

I told her that I didn't get them and now I'm in Cali on my way to Atwater. She told me that she looked up USP Victorville and wanted me to stay there and asked how I could make it happen, blah, blah, blah. I told her again that I was just being held over at USP Victorville and that I was being shipped on the next bus to USP Atwater.

She had plans on staying with my mom for two weeks but since I was no longer in Florida, she had to figure out what she was going to do.

We were going back and forth for a minute because she just popped up out of nowhere, expecting everything to be everything. She just found time to write me? I had been in the box for ten moons and all I received from her were two cards. She was never there when I needed her the most. How could she even consider calling herself my wife or even my girl for that matter? We really were going through it, going back and forth for the whole fifteen-minute phone call. I had to call her back in thirty minutes because the phone beeped. I looked up at the clock on the wall. I had forty-five minutes left before turning in for the night so I did five hundred push-ups and took a shower.

When I went to the computer to check my emails, Beauty had sent me ten emails. She was so happy to be in touch without having to wait on the mailman. I smiled. She put her number in all

105

the emails and asked me how much calls cost because she could send money to hear my voice. I put her number on my phone list, saying to myself "*I am calling her as soon as I come out of the cell tomorrow*".

I called my mother's number back and once mom answered and accepted the prepaid call she put Oceasia back on.

"What you going to do out there in Cali?" she asked.

"I'ma do my time," I replied.

"Don't be mad at me... You're the one who keeps going to the hole for investigations... you're the one who keeps getting in trouble... you got yourself transferred, not me."

"Yeah? ...Those same investigations I keep goin' under are for makin' sure you and everyone else is straight," I barked.

"Maybe you need to make sure you are straight instead of everyone else then," she quipped.

"You know what? That's what I'm going to do," I snapped.

After calming down and talking about her trip to Florida and enjoying my mother's company... the phone beeped.

"Can you call me back?" she asked.

"Nah... we gotta go in at two o'clock, which is in like five minutes."

"So call me tomorrow as soon as you come out Bae."

"Nah... I'ma email you... I got someone else I need to call. I got other calls to make."

"Why?" You need money or something?" she asked.

"Nah... I need to make some moves and let others hear my voice. I will email you." I told her.

"Who is she?" she asked.

"Not you." I said.

"She will never love you like me," she proclaimed.

I acted like I didn't even hear her.

The phone beeped again letting us know that the call was about to end in thirty seconds.

"I love you Shakim" she said.

I said ... "I love me too" as the call ended.

I emailed Oceasia as soon as I hung up. I had less than five minutes left before locking in for the day. As soon as I logged in and typed as quickly as I could with two fingers, this is what was sent:

Subject: "Master Equality" [ME]

You don't appreciate me.

You didn't even speak about the novel I wrote about our love.

You're never there.

You're everywhere else but where you need to be.

*   *   *

CHAPTER 13

The next day we didn't go out in the daytime as I expected. We went out at 8:30 that morning, meaning, we had until 11:30am to be out and about. I moved around a bit and went to build with Star & Amir, who were cellies. Star and I planned on working out together. I made my way to the computers to check my emails. I logged in and saw I had five emails from Beauty, three from Oceasia and a few from my comrades on the streets. As I opened up Beauty's email and read them, I planned on surprising her with a phone call even though I knew she was at work.

I opened up one of Oceasia's emails and the subject read "Foolish Fool" by Chaka Khan.

Make sure you forward this email to that chick you need to call so bad… let her know this came from me…

"She knows… she's crazy?

You know she got the wrong girl [Chaka talking]

[Chaka starts singing] "Foolish, foolish, foolish, foolish, foolish, fool if she thinks that she can take you away from me.

She got to be a foolish, foolish, foolish, foolish, foolish fool.

She gotta be crazy, crazy, crazy, crazy, crazy, crazy girl

if she thinks she can… destroy my world…

My love for you is too strong.

We've been together for too long.

She got to be a foolish, foolish, foolish, foolish, foolish fool

If she thinks she can take you away from me

She got to be crazy

[Chaka talking] she must not know who she is messing with.

After reading that, I laughed to myself but I made sure to I get that song as soon as I copped my MP3 so I could hear it, and read Oceasia's other emails.

"I need you to call me today… you can call her… just make sure you call me! 9-12-21."

I logged off and went looking for Star so we could do 45 minutes of Two Push-Up Burpees.

Star damn near killed me with his vicious work out. Afterwards, I went to use the bathroom and took a nice hot shower before making my way to the phones. It was ten minutes to ten in the morning when I dialed Beauty's cell number. After four rings her voicemail came on. I hung up and dialed her number again. After another three rings and I heard a female voice come on as the recording on my end started to play.

"This is a call from a Federal prison... this is a prepaid call... you will not be charged for this call... This call is from... ShaKim Bio... to decline the call please hang up... to accept the call, please press five now. To block any future calls from this inmate, press 7."

As she listened to the options and immediately pressed '5' I heard her say "Hello?" with her sexy voice.

"Beauty?... What's good, Ma?"

"Ooooh my gosh... ShaKim?"... I can't believe I'm really talking to you!" she said all so excited.

"Stop it, Ma... you know it's me. What's up with you, you see I called?"

I smiled, knowing she was happy to hear from me.

"I'm so happy right now that I may pee on myself... It feels so good to hear your voice and call me the name that you gave me. You know that's on my license plate now?"

"No doubt" I answered.

"I'm at work. You know I wasn't even supposed to be taking no calls. I can get in trouble," she spoke.

"Ok, look I'ma call you back," I tell her.

"No... No, talk to me. I can take a warning or a fine."

"Nah, Ma... I'm not going to put you through all that. I just wanted to call you, let you hear my voice. I wanted to hear

111

yours and let you know I was thinking about you," I said with my smooth baritone lol.

"I can't believe that I'm actually talking to ShaKim! When can you call me back?" she asked.

"We go in at 11:30am but we're three hours behind your time so I can't call back today. If we come out in the afternoon, I can hit you like 1pm or so… that will be 4pm your time."

"Ok. Just call me at 1pm your time. I'm going to take my lunch break then so I can talk to you babe and I'm going to email you everyday. You're going to wake up every morning to an early morning email from me" she promised.

"I hear you, Beauty."

"Nah, you're going to see me and know that I am feeling you ShaKim," she said, seriously.

"Ok then… we will see" I replied.

It felt so good to finally talk to Beauty. I was smiling. She made me feel real special. She was so happy and excited to talk to me. I remember when Oceasia use to act like that every time I called. I missed that but she pushed me to the next chick (Beauty) by not being there when I needed her.

I went to the computers to email my comrades and let them know I was journeying to USP Atwater. Thirty minutes had passed and I was able to place another phone call. I called my mother's cell number... after 3three rings I heard my mom's voice as she picked up.

"Hello?" The recording then came on and I could hear the '5' button being pressed.

"Peace Bae," my earth, Oceasia, addressed me. My ole earth [my mother] must have passed the phone to her.

"Peace," I answered.

"You calling early, I see."

"Yeah... we came out early today."

"Oh... and you didn't call her yet?" she asked sarcastically.

"Yeah... I did call. We spoke for a few minutes but she was at work."

It was quiet for a few minutes.

"Yeah?... You called her, huh? I hope she understands when she gets that email I asked you to forward to her."

I was quiet.

"How long are you going to be there? I found out how far you are from LA. You are two and a half hours from me so I need you to stay there and I'ma move back to LA so I can be closer to you and come see you every weekend" she proclaimed.

I didn't understand her saying that at all. When she was supposed to move to Florida, she moved to California instead. Then when I finally got transferred to Cali, she was back on the east coast. I have no time to be chasing her.

"Did you hear me Bae?"

"True indeed. I told you I'm waiting on the next bus to USP Atwater… that's where they got me designated to go. I'm just here on holdover status. See how far Atwater is from LA."

"Ok," she replied.

"Let me ask you this… how come you moved back to the east coast now that I'm finally in Cali but when I was on the east coast you moved out here? You expect me to stop what I'm doing whenever you feel like popping back up in the picture?" I had to ask her this.

"It's not like that. Evher's career is what moved me to Cali. I know I was supposed to have been come out this way. I know I am not doing what I'm supposed to or holding you down right and exact. I'm striving to get everything on point so we can have everything we need. I'm working on all that right now," she urged.

I didn't even want to argue with her. We've been at that point with the same argument so many times that I just got quiet, which should have said enough.

"I'm coming to see you. I'm coming back to California" she announced.

114

"Why did you leave? What happened to your apartment?" I asked.

She didn't answer.

"Where are you resting now?" I asked.

"I am staying in Atlanta now," she answered.

"Word?... Well, I am staying in California now so you are on the wrong coast, like always. You are never where you are supposed to be," I said, in a somewhat annoyed tone.

"At least I am trying" she said, light weight defending herself.

"Trying is not good enough, strive and make effort." I demanded.

"I came down here to see you. I miss you so much. I love you, ShaKim nothing can change that. I'm coming to see you. I'm bringing my daughter to see you in prison, when her own father never got to see her or hold her. I put you first over any man, even my father. No man can take your place or come before you. I love you ShaKim."

"Ok, I hear you Oceasia."

"Yeah. Born u truth [but] I need you to feel me and really believe me. You are my life and I truly love you regardless of whom or what" she spoke.

"I love you too, Ma" I replied.

115

I don't know what happened or where things went wrong but our relationship was not the same. I spoke to Oceasia everyday... sometimes three – four times a day and we emailed each other back and forth. I wrote her regularly, sent her cards, gifts, money, photos and I was in her daughter Evher's life as much as I was able to be. Things went the other way when I went to the box.

Oceasia didn't stay in tune with me. It's like our communication went dead but not on my end... only hers. She knew and overstood that I was locked up in prison and just about everything was unpredictable... the prison has been on numerous lockdowns, some lasted days, some lasted weeks... sometimes we were on lockdown for months at a time. I couldn't call, email or receive visits during lockdowns. In prison, I could end up in the box at any given time for any reason. I could lose any of my privileges just for being written up but to this day, I still know how to get around and maneuver to make things happen. Oceasia knew and overstood that [well, maybe she didn't] I shouldn't have had to stay on top of her to hold me down. She could reach out to me just like I continuously reached out to her and her family. There is a reason why she is slacking and not doing her duty, which is holding me down. I was at a point in my life and bid where I was tired of the let downs and disappointments. It's like she couldn't decide what she wanted to do or where she wanted to be so I wanted her to stay with whatever distraction she had and let me do me.

When we talked, we spoke about little things but overall the conversation was good. She kept telling me that she loved me and how she was a little down after she couldn't get to surprise

116

me with a visit. However, she was making the best of her visit to Florida; she had Evher with her and was enjoying the company of my two nieces so yea, Evher was good.

When the phone beeped, we knew our minutes for the call were up and I told her I would call back to speak with Evher.

"Ok, Bae... what time you calling?"

"In about understanding cipher [30 minutes)" I said.

"9-12-21."

"9-12-21," I repeated after her.

I had fun talking to Evher Peace. She was so intelligent for a seven year old. She was asking me a lot of questions too. That is my little young diva and I love her. It's crazy when I think back on all I went through in *Love, Hell or Right,* for me to still be on the phone talking to Evher. I probably got over 200 photos of her. Oceasia got back on the phone to tell me what she and my mother's plans were for the day. I told her that I may leave on a bus in the morning.

She told me that she had to go back to Atlanta to straighten out a few things then she was returning to New Orleans for a hot second before journeying to California to come see me.

"I will try to call you tomorrow if I'm still here" I said.

"Ok, Bae."

"9-12-21."

"Wait… your ole Earth wants to talk to you but make sure you speak to me before hanging up."

I spoke to Mom for a quick minute and she put Oceasia back on. She was truly enjoying Oceasia's company.

"Ok, Bae… hit me tomorrow if you are still there and email me."

"Ok"

"9-12-21" she said.

"All Day - Everyday," I replied.

Before locking in the cell for the rest of the day, I went to the computers to shoot Beauty a quick email.

Subject: Hearing your voice

The body of the email read:

"It was a pleasure to finally hear your voice and chat with you, even though it was short. I may leave in the morning and miss our date on the phone... plus I'm not going to play games or lie. I've been talking to my girl. She is in Florida right now at my mom's and had plans of visiting me but I got shipped.

Right now, we back and forth... you already know how it goes and how it went.

You read the novel... right? You know I love her and where I'm at with her.

If I'm still here, I'ma call you. If I don't call, that means I'm on my way to USP Atwater... 1

About 3am, we were woken up and told to get ready. We were getting ready to go to R&D. So I got up, got my hygiene on point and got myself together.

119

Around 4am, they came to escort us to R&D. There were about fifty convicts getting on the bus that would carry us to USP Atwater.

We were taken to R&D and fed a simple breakfast. It took about two and a half hours to strip us, search us, dress us in transit clothes then cuff and shackle us. I had to be "black-boxed" again. We had to wait for our names to be called and in turn, we stood up, stated our full names and register numbers then we were directed to form a line to get on the bus.

As we walked single file to the bus, we were given a brown paper bag with turkey and cheese sandwiches, peanut butter and jelly, pretzels and water. This was lunch. We were allowed to sit wherever we wanted so I made it over to a window seat. Star and Amir came over to where I was sitting. The air conditioning was on super-blast and everyone was freezing. I think they did that to make sure we were uncomfortable as possible, the toilet in the bathroom at the back of the bus didn't flush either. It was all good though, at least we were on our way to our destination.

It was a seven-hour ride because of the back road routes we were taking. We were passing so many cow farms. I'm so glad that I don't eat beef. The ride was so uncomfortable. Everyone on the bus was caught up in conversations. Somehow, some convicts managed to sleep through the cold air and bumpy ride on top of the nasty smell in the air.

Star and I built about our cases, other people's cases and comrades we both knew in our hometown (Queens) and shared other thoughts and positive moves. I told him about my second novel that I was planning to release soon. We built for hours and

120

some other convicts came in and out of our conversation. I, at one point, rested for an hour or so. Looking out the window, other than highway, I saw nothing but land and mountains... land and mountains.

Star and my convo paused for whatever reason and in a quiet moment to myself, I peered out the window, thinking to myself how these devils were (and still are) ill with how they place all these prisons way out where it's hard for families to visit regularly. Who's even heard of Atwater? I was going on twenty years of incarceration and them people still had me traveling the United States... through Federal prisons. I started shaking my head thinking about how my family's been through the ups and downs. At least, I'm still living but damn... a fellah been caged up for a while. I was taken out of my daze when Star asked...

"What's good?"

"Nothing... I'm just out there in thoughts... a little something." I revealed.

Star had the same skin complexion as me. He had short wavy hair, he probably 5 feet seven inches tall and was in great physical shape due to his dedication to working out, which was high on his list of priorities, second only to his legal battles with the courts.

"You were out there more than just a little something. You were way out there!" He stated as we started laughing.

"They got us way out here in Cali, Northern Cali at that. Who the fuck is going to come way out here to see me?" He asked.

121

"Shit is crazy, God. My Earth was in Los Angeles, only three hours away from Victorville," I said.

"Damn Sun!" Star reacted.

"Yeah... but check this... she is at my ole Earth's crib in Florida. She was coming to Coleman to visit me and now I'm way out here."

"Yeah Sha... that's crazy but at least you still got someone checking for you after twenty years so you gotta still be about something" he said.

"I guess so" I replied.

"You think she's coming up here past all these mad cow farms to come check on you again?" He wondered out loud.

"I trust that she will" I answered.

"You know she will, Sha. Shorty loves you. You wrote a whole novel about her. She better come up here, even if she has to walk"

We laughed.

I still couldn't help but wonder if Oceasia was still feeling me like that or what and where we stood then I thought about Beauty and began wondering to what degree she was feeling me? I put my head back and tried to enjoy the journey to USP Atwater.

"How Deep is Your Love?"

Keith Sweat

CHAPTER 14

USP Atwater was in a rural area, in a very small town where for the most part there was nothing but useless land. That's all I could see... land. No roads, no houses. All I saw was land and the air smelled like chicken shit, the only thing it had going was the federal prison. There was also a federal camp across from the prison.

We were called off the bus by name the same way we were called to board the bus. We had to give our full names, register numbers and birth dates then we were escorted inside the prison into R&D, where the cuffs and shackles were taken off and we went through the strip and search procedures to filled out forms and questionnaires. From there we went through a process of interviews with medical staff, case managers, counselors, the psychology department and the captain's review then we were told where we would be housed. This process took over three or four hours, maybe a little longer.

By the time I was given a bedroll, two sheets, two blankets, one wash cloth and a towel, I was exhausted. I went to Unit 1A, Star and Amir went to 3B but we were all on the same side of the prison's compound. The yard and units were set up just like Victorville and Coleman's yard. There were three buildings on each side of the yard but each building was split into two, two-story units, totaling six units on both sides. Each unit held one hundred-thirty to one hundred-fifty convicts. The yard was in the middle and it consisted of a quarter mile track, four basketball courts, two handball courts, two boocie balls and two horseshoe pits, a softball field and a football field that was also used as a soccer field. The yard was fenced in and each rec yard was split in threes so you could either go to the softball field, basketball courts [where the handball courts were] or to the trackside.

The prison was separated, meaning if you were housed on one side, you couldn't mingle with convicts housed on the other side. So it was like being in two prisons even though there were ways to get to one side or the other. The unit I was housed in was built just like Coleman and Victorville's on the inside also. As I stepped into the block everyone on the ground floor was looking at me. There were convicts on the second tier, leaning on the rail looking down, some were mean mugging, some were looking for a familiar face - either friend or foe and I was doing the exact same things. There was no question that I was a new arrival with the R&D pants, tight white t-shirt and blue karate shoes on, carrying a bedroll under my arm.

"ShaKim Bio-Chemical" I heard my name being called and I turned to see who it was. It was my manz "Black" from Washington, D.C., I was in USP Big Sandy with him from March 2005 to December 2006.

"Black... what's good?" I gave him a pound with my right fist.

"You... you Sha. I heard you were doing some good things in Florida" He exclaimed.

"Like what?" I inquired.

One thing about the Fed system that never fails is convicts get the gossip through the wire and most of it is blown out of proportion.

"I heard you got like eight novels out and you signed with either Teri Woods or Wahida Clark... some say you signed with both."

I got a good laugh out of that.

"Nah, I put one novel out with this small self publishing company, it ain't nothing major yet." I assured him.

Black was dark-skinned with short hair that he kept under his doo rag. He had the seasick waves. He had a medium build, probably weighed about one hundred-ninety pounds and he wore designer glasses.

"You know I know you Sha. You probably sold the same book twice to both of them" we laughed. "Yo, let me find you a cell. You already know how shit is out west and how they rock."

"Yeah, I was out here in Cali back from 2000 to 2002 when Lompoc was a pen." I reminded him.

Out in California, shit was run differently than most pens. There was nothing but gang bangers... every gang you could think of was there; Bloods, Crips, GD's, Vice Lords, Latin Kings, PIASAS, Surenoes Mexican gangs, MS-13 to, Netas and G27's. So the cells were geographical to Crip cells, Blood cells, East Coast cells, Mexican cells, Down South cells, DC cells to Midwest cells, to the section where they sat at to watch the TV they controlled, where they sat at in the chow hall.

Everything seemed laid back but would go from zero to 1000 in a split millisecond. There was a respect code that

126

everyone tried to follow and there was a lot of politics / "poli-tricks" going on just to keep the peace so I had to find an East Coast cell to stay in.

Black showed me where DC (District of Columbia dudes) sat and where the East Coast convicts sat to watch the TV they ran. Anybody could watch any TV but you had to sit behind the group who section you were in and you couldn't disrespect them by turning the television or taking over their table or seating arrangements.

I was introduced to a lot of convicts who asked where I was from, how many dudes came off the bus with me, where they were from and how many homeboys came with me. These questions were asked everywhere in the Fed system when a new arrival came in. I was familiar with a lot of convicts in that unit from other pens. This was the seventh pen I'd been in since entering the federal system. Convicts came to greet me and give me hygiene supplies or little food items. That is how it mostly goes; when you arrive at a new spot, you get supplies from the convicts who know you from your home state. They get you a little bit of stuff to hold you over until you either make it to the store or your property comes but I've seen where dudes don't give up nothing. I'm glad I was likable and known.

My celly's name was Penny, he was from Mount Vernon, New York, which is kind of a hood / suburb area of Westchester County just north of New York City and just above the Bronx. Penny and I chopped it up for most of the night as he was putting me on point and bringing me up to speed on what was going on at USP Atwater.

127

From what he was telling me, I knew a lot of the "NY home team" there as well as other convicts who I'd been doing time with in other institutions. It was different pens but mostly the same faces. It just so happened that my celly was also the unit's store man and he had just about every thing. I took what I needed and let him know I would pay him as soon as I touched the store and acquired prison compound money, which in the feds is in the form of United States postage stamps. I played no games when it came to adjusting and getting myself on point. My celly also worked in food service. He went back to work around 3am so after a while, I let him fall back and get his well needed rest in as I got situated.

Around 3am a C.O. came to wake up my celly so he could get ready for work at food service. I was on the top bunk so I stayed there to give him his space to move around and get his hygiene ready. Once he had himself on point, he explained how he ran his store so if I wanted to, I could hold him down while he was at work. I told him that I would do what I could but I may be busy moving around. Whatever stamps he made or had available, I was gonna buy from him anyway so either way it was a win-win situation for him and me. We dapped up and he rolled out, the C.O. locked the cell door and I laid back down to get my thoughts together. My computer and phone would both would be on that day and I had a lot to do.

At 5:45am, a C.O. began opening up the cell doors. I was already up, ready and on point and as I came out the cell when I bumped into another convict that I knew from Coleman 2. His name was Money Roy. He was from Miami, FL. We built for a minute on what was going on in Coleman since he left and he put me on point about Atwater. He asked if I was good… if I needed anything. I told him I was good.

"Nah… I'm going to hit you with a few things anyway," he insisted as he went towards the stairs that led up to the second tier. I looked around noticing the early risers and noticed that there were a lot of Mexicans moving around. Money Roy came back and handed me several books of stamps.

"I ain't doing all that good but here's fifteen books so you can do you" said Money Roy.

"Good looking… I was going to get right regardless" I stated as I tried to hand him back the stamps.

"Stop that Bio… that's you," as he pushed my hand back.

"No doubt… no doubt… Yo Roy, let me ask you something."

"What's up, God?" he asked.

"Yo, what's up with all these Mexicans?"

He started laughing. "Yo, you ain't seen shit yet… that's all you are going to see… Mexicans, nothing but Mexicans, Mexican C.O.'s and everything" Roy alerted.

"Word?"

"Shit... They love your celly. That's all your celly fucks with at his store... Mexicans and white boys, you would think he was Mexican."

"Wow" was all I could say.

At about 6:20am, they called "mainline" which was the move to go to breakfast. Sound travels at 1,120 feet per second so when I stepped out of the unit, there were already convicts I knew standing out on the walkway waiting on me.

"Peace to the true and living God" Ra-mega shouted.

I smiled when I saw Ra-mega who I hadn't seen since 2003, when I was in USP Lee County in Virginia. The God still looked the same but his dreads were way longer, we dapped and embraced.

"Peace to the God," I greeted.

"No standing still on the walkway!" a C.O. shouted.

"Let's motivate God," Ra-mega spoke as I stepped with him.

"Peace to the God... I come in the divine attribute of Sincerely Mathematics God Allah."

"Peace my name is King Jahzerah Allah Mathematics."

"Peace to the God, you already know who this is"

We all laughed at the God Jahkee from Boston, who was with me in Coleman.

"Man, we must build, Sha... it's a super- must" urged Jah-kee.

"True indeed," I replied.

"Nah ShaKim... Real talk, we gotta build," protested Jahkee, whose dreads had also grown longer since the last time I saw him.

As we were walking towards the west corridor building, instead of going to the chow hall, I was going to laundry first to pick up my clothes. When I entered laundry and gave all my clothes sizes, I was told to come pick them up at 7:30 am. Mexican C.O.'s ran laundry and most of the C.O.'s I had seen so far were Mexicans.

"Yo, Sha," said Ra-mega. "You got a Jamaican homeboy who runs laundry so he is going to lace you up when you go back. He comes to work around 7am and already knows that you are here."

"True indeed," I responded.

"Yeah, mad heads know you're here," said Jahkee. "Your manz 'J' got a welcome to Atwater bag for you with new sneakers, gear, food and all."

"Jay?" I questioned. "What Jay?"

"Damn Jahkee... you wasn't supposed to tell Sha," quipped Ra-mega.

Ra-mega was six feet two inches, had brown skin with an athletic build. The God was from Connecticut but caught his case in

Richmond, Virginia. He was very, very swift with his math and was a great builder. I spoke on him and used one of his builds in *Love, Hell or Right.*

"He speaking on your peoples Jay, that tall brown-skinned, Jamaican cat from Brooklyn."

"Word? That's my peeps... Jay from the nineties in Flatbush." I know Son very well. We were in Coleman together.

"Yeah, him... and the Yardman got mad shit for you" bragged Jahkee, who was five feet eleven with a husky build and a shade lighter than me. Jahkee's dreads were now down to his shoulders, while Ra-Mega's were past his lower back so when he sat down he might sit on his dreads.

Sincerely Mathematics, whom everyone called "Math" for short, was an understanding seed [light-skinned] and was built like a football player with a big broad chest. He had a crispy baldhead and was from Elizabeth, New Jersey. New Jersey was also known as "New Jerusalem." I knew of his case and a few of his codefendants. His "co-dee", Amir, was my manz and his other co-dee, Corey, was well known in the Feds. Math was also a chess champ. He carried his rolled up chessboard in his tote bag and stayed looking for action.

King Jahzerah was a wisdom seed (brown-skinned) and was also built like a linebacker. He looked like he had been lifting weights his whole life. He also had a crispy baldhead. For some reason, they called Jahzerah "Hoffa" but I soon found out he was super swift with his math as well and like the rest of them, knew and understood 120 and was ready to show and prove at the drop of a hat. It was real peace to be around Universal Builders.

On the way into the chow hall, I bumped into convicts that I knew from different pens. The chow hall was very geographical. You had to sit in the section with whomever you ran with. If you were from New York but was on Blood time (a Bloods gang member), then you sat with the Bloods and not New York. Same if you were from St. Louis and ran with the Crips, you wouldn't sit in the Midwest section because you were on Crip time. You could stop and holler in any section but that section was reserved for those who ran and repped that cause to the fullest. It was very important that everyone moved with respect or shit would get out of hand with the spill of bloodshed. USP Atwater was on gang banging time.

I met most of the East Coast home team as well as the New Yorkers and was I introduced to the New York Bloods on the strength of them being from NY. Atwater was filled with poli-tricks / politics.

On the way out of the chow hall I made sure to get a commissary list so I could hit up the store and blow my whole spending limit on everything I knew I would need; an MP3 being one of the things I needed asap. I'd been hearing so much about MP3's. They just came out while I was in the box in Coleman. It was a must that I have one. I wasn't surprised that they allowed us to have MP3's in the Feds. It was needed in this tense environment where we could listen to the music that we particularly liked instead of listening to the radio and the songs they kept in rotation that play over and over again all day long.

With an MP3, we could get the songs we liked and that would brighten moods in a spot where attitudes were fucked up most of the time.

I also noticed, unlike USP Coleman, Atwater did not have a lot of females working. I was so used to seeing Black or Spanish women, all day in Coleman, but now all I was seeing was one here and there [Mexican] but no doubt, Mexicans ran this spot.

The prison was separated, but we were allowed to mingle together on the rec yard. There were three rec yards... from 7:30am to 2:30pm we were allowed to mingle together. After the 2:30pm recall, we were separated until the next day but the west end ate with the west end and the east end ate with the east end. Every day, we were separated after 2:30pm as well as weekends and holidays.

I guess this was a great science experiment that someone way up top in the Bureau of Prison's top brass had come up with because this project was introduced to USP Atwater first and once it was proven to be tried and true, the concept started being implemented in most of the other USP's.

What's so crazy was if you were in one building and wanted someone in another, the way they ran the institution and kept y'all separated, was like y'all were on two different prison compounds. When in reality, y'all were both in the same prison.

As the years went by, it only got worse so the MP3 move was definitely a plus for those who were forced to live in this reality.

I made it back to laundry to pick up my institutional clothes and also got to meet the Jamaican homeboy I was told about. His name was "Jah-B" from Brooklyn. We built for a while and learned that we knew a lot of the same people on the streets. He was Jamaican born but New York raised and also part of the founding members of the Blood movement in New York. That was the reason he was in the Feds. He was about a five foot eight inch, wisdom seed [brown-skinned] and weighed about one hundred and seventy-five pounds with an athletic build. He kept his dreads in a Rasta crown and was the type who read a lot of books, ranging from philosophy to religion, history of wars and empires. He was deep yet if you stood around for too long, you might begin think just maybe he knew too much and the shit was making him crazy. Overall, he was a good dude.

"Yo Bredden… Jay speaks highly of you. We going to get you moved over to our side in our unit so you can vibe with us and we can build more. I see you sharp on your sword as well." He said in a low broken Jamaican accent with New York slang.

"Yeah, no doubt. Jay's my dude" I said.

"I also hear you're the one who wrote that love story that all the Five Percenters in here got. Jay just bought the novel."

"Did you read it yet?" I asked.

"No. I don't read those love story kind of novels."

"How come Jah B?" I asked.

"Because. I'm not in love. I'm of love... plus me and my Queen read books together so we can both add on in discussion about it. I'm hearing too much that will maybe cause confusion in my house... so, nah... that's not what I think I'll be having my Queen reading!"

We both laughed.

"But I'm going to order the novel and read it without my Queen" he said as we smiled and dapped up.

"Yo, I put extra gear in the bags for you. I made sure you got extra everything and you done know that everything new God - seen!"

Jah-B let it be known that he runs laundry and not the Mexicans who ran everything else.

"Let me know if you need a job detail too" he said as we pounded fists.

"No doubt!" I responded.

After I made it to commissary and blew my whole spending limit, I dropped off all my stuff and fixed up the cell a bit while waiting on the rec move so I could go on the yard to meet up with Jay. I made sure that I had everything I needed because my spending limit revalidated within a week and trustfully my property would have arrived. "Black" came through to check on me.

"Damn Sha... those Teri Woods and Wahida Clark book checks must be lookin' lovely!" Black said as we laughed.

136

"Yo remember Eyeone Williams that was in Lee County with you?" He asked me.

"Yeah. I remember Son. I heard he is doing big things out there with his novels from Fast Lane to Lorton Legends. I read most of his shit, what's up with him? I asked as Black handed me a piece of paper.

"I spoke to him and told him you were here. He said to pass you his number so you could call him. He is doing well and about to start doing short films." Black said as I accepted the piece of paper and put it in my pocket.

"Good looking," I said.

"Yo. Some dudes were looking for you... like 10 to 12. They were eager to see you too. More of the on the love tip... not no ill foe type shit" Black said putting me on point. "I think they were your NY homies from the other side... they came through like an hour or so ago. One of them hollered at Money Roy," he informed me.

"Ok. Good looking. Yo, later on I need you to show me how to activate my MP3."

"Got you one now, huh?" he asked.

"No doubt," I answered.

"That's what I'm talking about... those book deals you played on both ends got you on top" assumed Black.

"Black... Believe me I ain't nowhere with this novel shit... yet." I said.

137

"You know I know you on something big... just keep me in mind... I will be there" "Black" assured me.

"No doubt," I replied as we pounded fists.

CHAPTER 15

Money Roy came to my cell twenty minutes later, he had two commissary bags full of food, a brand new sweatshirt and sweat pants and brand new sneakers.

"Yo Bio, your manz Jay came over here mad deep looking for you. He left these two bags for you. I see you at it already" he stated as he left the bags in the middle of the cell's floor.

"He said that he will be on the rec yard waiting on you so make it out there on the next move" said Money Roy.

"Ok, good looking out" I said as we pounded fists.

I made it to the computers and stood in line so I could check my emails, which should have been activated. I expected my phone to be on as well. The line for the computers was like a fifteen minute wait so I told dude in front of me to hold my spot until I came right back. I went to lace up the brand new Nikes that Jay sent me then I got back in line and waited my turn.

When my turn came up, I logged in and I had over 20 emails. "Beauty" got at me real heavy but Oceasia left me most of the emails. I read as many as I could but didn't respond to any. I was going to give them both a call after 4pm. Knowing Cali was three hours behind east coast time. I checked my watch for the time. It was almost 9am so I logged off and got ready for the 9am rec move to the yard.

Once I made it to the yard, Jay was sitting on the steel picnic table with numerous convicts sitting or standing around him. I smiled because he hadn't changed a bit. I walked over to him and he stood up and gave me a pound fist handshake and embrace.

"Bredden, what's good?" he asked.

"Me, I'm good" I responded.

"I shot mad shit to your unit for you. I gave it to Money Roy" Informed Jay.

"No doubt. Good looking… I got that" as I looked down at my feet causing him to look down. "Plus you already know I touched the store and blew my limit" I added as we laughed.

Jay introduced me to most of the NY homeboys and Jamaicans. Jay was a Jamaican shot caller from Brooklyn, New York, who got trapped off in a weed conspiracy that gave him thirty years in the Feds. We were in Coleman together and we were tight because of our Jamaican and New York backgrounds. We both made moves that made differences.

"Yo, call Mom Dukes up and let her know you are here with me" Jay playfully ordered.

"Nah, you call her yourself" I said.

We laughed.

"About time you came outside" an unfamiliar voice said that caused me to spin around.

Standing there was a knowledge seed [dark-skinned], He was 6'3" with a slim build, clean, long thin dreads that almost hung to the back of his calves. We stood there looking at each other as the others stood around watching us. I was trying to place his face as he smiled at me.

I looked again... Nah, it can't be... but it was him.

"Qasim," I responded as we gave each other a brotherly hug. I hadn't seen him since November 1993, a month before I got hemmed up.

Qasim was one of the main reasons Irv Gotti was discovered. He gave Irv a chance to showcase his talent as a DJ back in the day. Qa was known for his fighting skills and was respected throughout Hollis, Queens. He was very good friends with the Antney brothers, who were known throughout Queens in the underground, hustler world. Now, they were in the entertainment industry. Their nephew was the rapper, "Waka Flocka Flame" and their sister, Debby, was Waka's mother and once upon a time, Nicki Minaj's manager.

"Yo, wait until I call Irv's brother, Chris, and tell him ShaKim Bio-Chemical is here" he said as we both smiled. Qa got hit with over 10 life sentences and still stood tall while fighting for his freedom.

"No doubt" I responded.

The New York and East Coast homies were very tight-knit. We talked laughed and joked.

"Yo, I heard your novel was doing numbers" said Qasim.

"Nah, Qa... shit is moving like a turtle" I answered.

"Yo, you the one who penned Love, Hell or Right?" asked another convict from New York.

"Yeah, that be him" responded Jay.

"Word!! I read that joint. That shit was the truth, my girl loved it" acknowledged the NY homie as Jah-kee, Star, Rah-Mega, Math and Hoffa made their way towards us.

Within twenty minutes we were in a heated debate. It started with my novel then we discussed what men in prison are looking for in a woman.

"Your novel opened the eyes to a lot of females on what we be going through in these struggles of prison life" said the NY homie.

"But nah, it don't apply to all dudes though. Some heads couldn't overstand your position or could relate to your situation" said Rah-Mega.

"Some females don't realize when they have a very good dude who's worth the world to them... they're so used to being taken advantage of and run over that they don't recognize and appreciate realness in a man when they see it" proclaimed Star as some dudes agreed.

"They so caught up in that Love and Hip Hop reality shit, which is really fantasy. Dudes got females caught up in so much... dramatizing over a fella" said Math.

"Shit, everyone wishes to have fine females to dramatize over them" said the NY homie.

"That's some real shit" Star said, agreeing.

"Yo, Sha… that's what I wanted to build with you about, God. That novel… it got my young girl open. She never knew Mathematics was that unique until you simplified it in your story and she likes how you and your Earth shined together, sharing letters and poems" Jah-kee added.

"Yeah… that sucker for love shit" Qasim joked and everyone laughed.

"Nah, for real… a real woman, who understands this struggle, will love and appreciate your novel. You spoke from a real dude's point of view" Jah-kee stated adamantly.

"Yeah, plus you didn't use no kind of derogatory words to down play or disrespect women, us, or our culture" added Rah-Mega.

"No calling women bitches or hoes or any of that other shit. You kept it in a real positive light. I know your Earth really appreciates you Sun." Jah-kee said, making an assumption.

I smiled because only if they knew the real and what I was going through with my Earth at that very moment…

"Yo, what was so ill about your novel was you let it be known and understood that all relationships go through changes, hardships, get tested and go through all kinds of hell to come out right" revealed Star.

"I hear you on that but personally, I couldn't have gone through all that. I got too many women on deck to go through all that soap opera shit with one. You seen how shorty got grimey on my manz by coming up pregnant?" Jay asked.

"Yo, it took a lot to write about that huh, God?" asked Star.

"Nah... I just was man enough to put it on paper when others wouldn't speak on shit like that at all," I said, looking around at not one in particular but knew some of the fellas felt I was targeting them.

"What does a female really want from a man in prison?" asked Mathematics. "I mean, I be going through it with my wisdom every now and then. I give her mad space to do her. I'm trapped off with a life sentence and that's my reality until I can change it but what does a female really want? You got dudes here who were mad real with their women, took care of them and all and still came up short once they came to prison. What do they want? Why then get upset and blame us for shit we can't control? All we want and need is for them to be there in some way. It be the little things that make us happy in here. A letter every now and then... photos... words of encouragement, emails... a visit." Math alluded.

"Shit... all my shorty had to do was press '5' and give me fifteen minutes... I'm cool with that!" Jay stated and some dudes laughed.

"Some females can't even keep it real to even do just that" added Qasim.

"Some females deserved to be called derogatory names like bitches and hoes. Look how they be doing us real cats" said Math.

"What about the ones who were mistreated and dogged by some of us so called real ones? We were miss-educating them, not preparing them for shit like this. Men are supposed to be a woman's provider, maintainer and protector but we were on some other shit out there too so we can't just put the blame on them. We're guilty too" Hoffa said.

"But what do they expect? If they met us on the block and we were doing our thing or we met them in the club, they already knew what we were about and what it was" said Qasim.

"But after they know all this, you knew this too and still chose to make her your girl or baby momma so you're definitely the blame" Hoffa pinpointed that factor.

"What do these women want from us?" asked Star.

"You said it yourself Hoff, they want a provider, maintainer, someone to protect them... they want to feel secure... they want to be loved, assured and reassured that their man truly loves them. A woman wants a real man, like how we want a real woman. If you don't want a chick to play games... you can't play games" Rah-Mega added.

"True... true but most of us were in the streets and living that life" said Jay.

"So that means you were looking in the wrong places" replied Hoffa.

"A man in prison needs a woman to be there... especially when he is at his lowest or weakest point. He needs her to help him stand tall. This shit aint as hard as it seems but some females choose not to do this bid with us" said Rah-Mega.

"ShaKim, what do you think is a good situation? You wrote the novel" asked a Brooklyn New Yorker, who was standing in our cipher.

"Buy the novel and read it. He got solutions in there. Just don't be no sucker for love type of dude like he was" Jay replied, some dudes laughed.

"Yo, God, why did you name the novel Love, Hell or Right? Show and prove and break that down for me." Jay said, attempting to put me on the spot because he liked to hear me build.

I smiled because of his apparent craftiness but also because of the opportunity to build and network. I dropped it with no problem...

"Love, Hell or Right is representing the twelfth letter in our supreme alphabet. Love has many different meanings but I'm bringing out the meanings that hold value... for love is the highest elevation of understanding... it is having a profound tender, passionate affection for another person; a feeling of warm personal attachment or deep affection for a parent, child or friend. Love "borns" power-culture all being born to Born so that shows that from love... things come into being" I stated as I looked around at the brothers who were truly paying attention to my words.

I continued...

"Hell is any place or state of torment, misery or something that causes torment or misery. It is extreme disorder, confusion and chaos. It is to be unpleasant to or painful for. Hell is the trick. We all go through hell. Hell borns understanding-God, borning knowledge cipher all being born to knowledge. Once you understand self as God and go through knowledge to cipher, you come into the true being and definition of self, which is knowledge. So having no knowledge at all is equivalent to being in Hell... "Or" is used to connect words, phrases or clauses representing alternatives like otherwise or else... or borns understanding-understanding all being born to equality."

"Right is to be in accordance with what is good, proper or just. In conformity with fact, reason, truth or some standard or principle, correct in judgment, opinion or action. Right borns equality-wisdom all being born to Build"

I stated as I stared at everyone in my midst.

"Sha, you got to be a walking dictionary to spit all that so easily," spat Jay as others laughed. "One thing I got to say about you is - you stay true and living. I just came in in

2008. I didn't see Gods out there building like they were in the 80's and keeping the teachings alive. It's like the Blood movement took over and the poor righteous teachers weren't a factor no more."

"Poor righteous teachers will always be a factor in the ghettos of America. A lot of our youth don't have fathers or father figures and they get drawn into the brotherhood that the Blood movement represents but without having knowledge of self, you will self-destruct... kill each other, kill self or end up in these hells. You heard the definition of hell." Proclaimed Rah-Mega.

"What I don't understand is what women really want from us? Even though we are trapped off in these hells, we are real with ours. What do women really want from a man who is locked up?" inquired Star, who was still ready to debate further.

"She wants a man who will listen and pay attention to her so when she explains or talks about her problems, he can come with solutions. A woman wants honesty, someone who will really keep shit official with her. She doesn't want much. She knows men on the outs be full of shit. It's rare to find a real, good, man who works hard man and has values and morals. They don't have much to choose from out there, a woman can't raise a boy into a man. Most men out there are still little boys in a lot of ways. The real good men are either in the graveyard or in prison" stated Hoffa.

"Ok but what do most of these men, who are locked up, want from a woman?" asked Star.

"Shiiiit. All I need is for a chick to send me money! Other than that I don't need shit from her". Exclaimed the Brooklyn rebel who was a young minded, young acting convict who really didn't give a fuck.

"That's what fucks it up for the ones who are serious about keeping it real with us. Dudes like him, who to take advantage of females" Star nodded his head in the rebels direction, indicating that he was speaking on him.

"Yo, all I need is for a shorty to keep it official with me. I need a real woman, who knows what she wants in life and knows how to get it and can hold her man down" Rah-Mega said.

"True... true. I need a female to have my back and give me support, and no... I'm not talking about financial support either" Hoffa stated as he looked over at the Brooklyn rebel.

"ShaKim... you wrote that novel... so what you want from your shorty?" asked Jay.

"All I want is her loyalty, her honor and her respect" I replied.

"Word!" agreed Rah-Mega, as others thought about what I said and nodded their heads in agreement.

"If I can't get that... I don't want nothin' else. Those things may sound simple but most women act like they can't even live up to that.

"Loyalty, Honor and Respect." I repeated.

*   *   *

CHAPTER 16

It was a little chilly outside but still the rec yard was crowded on all 3 yards. There was a lot going on. You saw fractions of Mexicans in groups working out and convicts of ever color doing the same thing. All the basketball courts had full court games going on. The sky was bright and blue and it was the middle of November. Back on the east coast most people were bundled up and dressed for cold weather but out here in northern California, it was a chilly fifty something degrees, not too cold, it was enjoyable.

Jay explained how the yard was run and how the prison compound carried itself. We were in "Gangland" but nevertheless, we were strong and made ourselves known and respected. Jay was in the same unit as Rah-Mega. Jah-B was his celly but Jay was going to make some moves to get a cell from one of the Mexican shot callers by either buying a cell or switching a cell in another unit to accommodate a cell within the unit so I could move from my unit to the unit Jay, Jah-B, and Rah-Mega were in. He explained that he had that move in the works so I had to start on my end by talking to my unit team about moving from my side of the prison compound to the other. I let him know that I appreciated that and I was definitely on top of that as soon as I got back to the unit. I dapped up all the home team comrades and went in on the ten-thirty yard recall. We all said we would link back up on the rec yard after lunch.

As soon as I made it back to the unit, I went to my assigned cell with Penny, grabbed my new MP3 player and got in the long line for the four email computers. Penny was in from work so I gave him space to do what he had to do in the cell but he came over to tell me that he was going back to the kitchen.

"I just came back to drop off these raw chicken parts" informed Penny. He still had a hustle going on even though we were locked up.

"Yo, I came in and saw all those bags of food and stuff. What, you trying to start a store?" he joked.

"Nah... I ain't trying to compete with what you got. Yo, give me the info to where you want me to shoot paper for some stamps" I said.

"How many you need?" He asked.

"How many you have to spare?" I answered with a question.

"Fuck it. I will give you 75 books for $200 cause you a homie" Penny said as he went to go write the info and also retrieve the stamps. 75 books were equivalent to $300. I needed that to move around with.

When my turn on the computer came up, I connected my MP3 player to the outlet plugs and logged in.

I saw that I had 17 email messages but instead of reading my emails, I clicked on the music option to activate my device. After going through the process, I searched for certain songs. I

152

was only allowed to buy fifteen songs a day so I had to choose my first fifteen, wisely. No doubt my very first song was Alicia Myers "I Want to Thank You." That's my shit! My second song was "Rising to the Top" by Kenny Burke. Then I got "Fool's Paradise" by Melisa Morgan. I wanted to get all old school joints but had to add a few Hip Hop songs so I went through Jay-Z, then Nas songs and picked the last twelve out of those two spitters. After downloading the fifteen songs, which I did everyday, I now had over 1200 songs in my MP3 player. I went to read my emails.

I got a few emails from my comrades and two from my co-partner of the publishing company. I read and responded to them promptly. Oceasia definitely got at me. She sent over ten emails, which I read but didn't respond back to. Beauty sent me two. One message let me know that she waited for my call but being that I didn't, she understood that I must have left for northern Cali. She told me to get at her whenever I had a chance. The other message was just letting me know that I was being thought of and I definitely appreciated that. No drama... no nothing. I didn't even reply back to her emails, instead, I called her.

"Damn celly... you just got here and you tryna bounce already?" Penny asked as he peeped me filling out the request form to be moved to the other side of the prison's compound.

"Yeah Sun. I gotta go on the other side of things with my peoples" I replied.

153

"You could stay on this side and still hang with your peeps all day. I don't have any one to rock with on this side, especially in the block. You need to stay over here. Ain't no NY homies in the block with me, Sun" said Penny, trying to persuade me.

"Damn... that's ill", I thought to myself. Penny was in the block by his self and even though he was by himself before I got there, now that I am here, I couldn't leave him over there by himself like that. I knew better and knew how the politics of prison life go.

"Ok, give me a minute on that" I replied.

"What's up?" he asked.

"Let me bring this up with my peeps on the other side... I may stay on this side" I informed.

"Word... plus you a cool and real dude so I wouldn't mind you staying" Penny said.

After chow I went to the rec yard on the first move. I saw Jay and crew and greeted everyone with pound handshakes.

"Yo Jay, let me chat with you for a second" I hollered as Jay and I took a walk around the track.

As we were walking we passed convicts in groups and some solo all caught up in their own little worlds, doing what they do to pass time. Some were selling sodas; others had old issues of Curve Magazine and a few Maxima magazines. Most of the yard peddlers were Mexicans. As Jay stopped to look at a Curve magazine, we began to chat.

"Wha gwaan Breddren? Everyting crisp?... You need anything?" he asked.

"Nah. Everything is everthing, Jay. Yo, Penny wants me to stay over there with him. He said there's no homies in the block with him" I said.

"Word... he on that now? There wasn't none over there before you came either." Jay responded.

"I know but shit is different now" I added.

"Look... I already got the cell. You my peoples and I trust and fucks with you hard body. I'ma grab the cell and move you in" Jay insisted.

"What about Penny? He's by himself" I reminded him.

"He came in this world by himself and he's gonna die by himself" we laughed at Jay's remark.

"Nah. I got a remedy for Sun" he added.

"What?" I asked.

"I'ma send one of the homies on our side over there so he can't complain about no homies in the block with him... that's that" Jay said smiling.

"Whatever. Just make it happen" I said.

"Yo... what's good with your Earth though, y'all still official?" Jay asked as we started walking again.

I then gave him a quick run down on the situation - Oceasia not being there when I need her, how she always gets lost, and I told him about the growing friendship I had with Beauty.

"Sounds like another situation like you had with Tammi" he replied.

"Nah. Because me and shorty really don't have no real history. I don't really remember her but we cool and she been getting at me super heavy" I said.

"Word?"

"Yeah. True story." I answered.

"So what you going to do my yout? You can't dead your shorty. Y'all suppose to be official. You got her name tatted on you and she is your heart but you can't dead the other shorty either, for she is there and may be what you really need. So hold on to her and let shit play out however it's gonna go."

"Nah," as I thought about it. "I can't do that cause I'ma be leading both of them on."

"We in prison my yout... we can't lead them nowhere. They know where we at and chose to fuck with us but at the same time don't think either of them ain't doing them. What you think the real reason the Earth is always getting lost? She is doing her my G" Jay said.

I had to smile because Jay swore he knew the nature of women and how they work but he always seemed to keep women nonstop problems.

"I tell you what... Get the Earth on the dance floor and ask her what's up and what it is... see what she says... that's the only way you are going to know for sure... get it from her face to face." Jay suggested.

"Now, I'm feeling that," I responded.

"And until you sort shit out, keep the other shorty. You can't dead her when your Earth ain't on her J.O.B.... Yo, ShaKim, you too fly for all that bullshit. Do what you do. You know how to move in these jungles. The Earth is messing up. She just don't know she got a real General, huh? Who she think you are... Homey the Clown?" Jay added, trying to joke about the situation.

"I can't call it, Sun" I responded. "But she knows I ain't him."

"These women be on some next shit with us real G's... they treat bosses like suckers!" Jay snapped, as we laughed.

"Just make sure you don't throw away a diamond for an empty sea shell God." He urged.

I thought about that jewel he threw me.

"Yo, I'ma get a homie over there to that block so you can move on this side with us" Jay said.

"No doubt" I responded.

*   *   *

CHAPTER 17

I made it back to the unit after 2:30pm yard recall and stood in line for the email computers. After about a fifteen minute wait, I finally got my turn. After logging in, I saw I had nine email messages. Four were from Oceasia, who was back in Georgia and wanted to know why I didn't send her my new address. I was thinking to myself *why would she want the new one when she never really put the old one to use like she was supposed to?* Then I read the messages from my street comrades. Beauty didn't send any emails. I guess she was going to wait until I got back at her. She was being real lady like and at the same time, wasn't pushing her limits. She knew full well that I had a woman. I responded to the other five emails, logged off and went to the phones to call my mother.

After dialing mom dukes number and entering my phone pac, I had to say my name at the beep. They had some new shit where your voice had to match the voice they had on your computer files. If not, the call would not go through. You had three tries before you had to hang up and try again. Technology was getting crazy back then and it's even crazier now. I said my name at the beep and it matched the voice on file.

"Your call is being processed," the female computer voice recording said. After three rings, my mother picked up. The recording came on telling her who was calling, that the call was from a federal prison and how to accept the prepaid call. She pressed '5' to accept the call.

"Hello?"

159

"Hi Mom, how are you doing?"

"Everything is fine. Where are you now?"

"I reached the new spot" I told her. "Get a pen so I can give you the address."

"Don't worry. Your girl supposed to call me back or text the address. She said she looked it up and got it" my mother informed me.

"Is that so?".

"Yeah. I enjoyed her and Evher's company. It was nice having them. They left yesterday," she said.

"Ok."

We spoke a while about the family home front and how everybody was doing.

"You ok over there? Do you need anything?"

"Nah. I'm cool. I went to the store and got what I needed and wanted plus, guess who is here?".

"Who?"

"Jamaican Jay," I said.

"Yeah? He is a nice guy. Tell him that I said hello. He sent me a card so I have to write him a thank him" she said.

"Yeah. You know how y'all yardie people are" I joked.

We spoke until the phone beeped letting us know our fifteen - minute call had come to an end.

"The phone just beeped so take care. I'll call you within a day or two Mom,"

"Boy, save your money. I'm going to be alright" she answered.

"I'ma call anyway to make sure."

"Ok. I love you son."

"I love you Mom. Give everyone my regards. Love you" I proclaimed.

We hung up.

After 4pm count, as soon as we were let out of our cells, I went to the phones to call Oceasia. It was about time I called. As I dialed her number, then input my nine number digit pac, I waited for the beep to say my name. After a few seconds, Oceasia's phone was ringing.

She picked up after four rings. She pressed '5' to accept the call.

"Peace Bay."

"Peace. How you? I see you made it back safely." I said to her.

"Yeah, I did. Why haven't you been responding to my emails?" She asked.

"For what? You don't give a fuck about me" I responded.

"What do you mean, I don't give a fuck?"

"You disappear and get lost and come around whenever you are ready. You are never there when I need you so I'm not going to continue to play your little games" I said.

"Whatever" she said.

"Exactly," I replied.

"ShaKim, it's not even like that... you are taking things the wrong way. I love you and you mean the world to me. I need you to fully overstand that. I don't want you to feel that way baby. Don't do this to me. I love you." Oceasia pled.

"You love me? Well you got a funny way of showin' it. Look, Oceasia, I have been through too much with you. I can't go through this shit again. It's either you are here with me or you are not. There is no in between. There is no jumping in and out then wanting to jump back in again. It's not going to work... not with master equality [ME]. You've got to make up your mind and stop being so indecisive. You have to make up your mind and stand on that." I demanded subtly.

"I am standing on it ShaKim. I love you all day everyday. Nonstop! It's always us Bae" she expressed.

162

"Then act like it then" I insisted. "You are on very thin ice with me right now. I'm so ready to walk away, Oceasia."

"Why?" she asks.

"Why? You just questioned me why? I can't believe this shit. You are asking me why. Tell me why should I stay" I replied.

"Because you love me... and I love you and we have the deepest love for each other. That's why" she responded.

"Well, if that is your answer and you say you stand on it... then how deep is your love?" I asked.

"Upgrade U"

Beyonce featuring Jay-Z

CHAPTER 18

That's the song that I'm listening to on my MP3 right now as I write this. I had to get that shit... shit is official. That's what I need... a female that will upgrade me. I don't need a "Beyonce" as far as looks, I mean, that would definitely be a plus but I need a woman with an entrepreneurial spirit like Beyonce'. A woman who is willing to build something that will last forever and leave traces of our legacy. I'm not looking for one to take care of me. I need her to motivate me to be better or should I say be 'greater'.

I finally got my property from Coleman so I was super good. I was heavy on food, sneakers and everything I needed. Jay also got me moved to his side of the prison. He got one of the NY homies moved over with Penny so everything was everything. At the moment, I had a cell to myself.

Jay and Jah-B would come hang out in my cell. We'd look through each other's photo albums and traded war stories. I also met this cat from Queens name "Latif" but we call him "Lah". He knew a lot of cats I knew from Queens. Lah was an understanding seed [light-skinned] with the Muslim groomed beard. You could tell he worked out excessively because he was 'diesel'. He was also one of those hard core Muslims who always spoke on Islam but once you got to know him and he was comfortable around you, he would open up and be on his Queens, NY shit. He was super-comical. He was full-blooded Jamaican but had been in the US since he was a baby. He had no accent and knew nothing about his native home. All he knew as N.Y. and what was so crazy was that he faced being deported back to Jamaica after he completed his sentence, which was under three years.

That was our crew in the unit - me, Jay, Lah and Jah-B.

Outside of the unit, it was Gangster Lou from Harlem, Star from Queens, Rah-Mega, Qasim, Jah-kee, Mathematics and Hoffa. There were still more New Yorkers that we messed with but that was the inner circle that was always around each other, especially after 2:30pm, now that we were all on the same side of the prison.

Me and Oceasia were back to flowing regularly. We talked on the phone once a day. I talked to Beauty weekly but that was about to change.

There were so many Mexicans at USP Atwater. Most of them were illegal immigrants that had no outside help so they hustled in prison to survive. One of their hustles was selling their phone minutes. The hard part was getting past the voice matching due to most of them having the funny Spanish names that were hard to pronounce with the Mexican accent. The wisest move was to have them dial the number, say their name and put the phone down and walk away once it started ringing then I would go over and pick up the phone like I was next in line. I had been mastering the imitating voice part so I didn't need to get them to clear the call. If you got caught up using another convict's phone, you could get a write up and lose all kinds of privileges so a lot of cats didn't fuck with the phones other than their 300 minutes. However, some like myself, needed several different phones to get shit done.

Three hundred minutes was not enough for me and plus someone put me onto this phone service that provided local area codes and phone numbers so when you called your family and loved ones, it was a local call instead of a long distance so instead of the twenty-three cents a minute, adding up to three dollars and forty-five cents for a 15 minute call, which was $69 a month, the local call was now six cents a minute totaling ninety cents a call... that's eighteen dollars a month. Using local numbers saved me fifty-one dollars, that meant more money to obtain more phone time from other Mexicans. You already know I was on top of that. I got most of my street team to look up these companies and paid the low fee to get the local number programmed to their phones. Oceasia had a local number and I was waiting on Beauty to get one too so I could have their numbers on their own lines, meaning I brought one Mexican's phone just for Oceasia and one just for Beauty. They both would have their own 300 minutes.

Other than that, Beauty and I flowed regularly through the email and she stayed writing me long letters and sending me cards.

I was also doing a lot of writing. I wrote a monthly column for Gorillaconvict.com, titled, "S.H.A.K.I.M's HOOD". S.h.a.k.i.m. is an acronym for Stop Holla And Keep it Moving". In the article, which I still write occasionally, wrote about prison politics / poli-tricks and prison life from all aspects. Some stuff I wrote was humorous, some was dead serious but all of them spoke on the reality of prison. I had a nice audience on there and also got to advertise my novels on the blog. They also interviewed me about my novel and posted on the site too. I was really doing a lot and feeling good about it.

Me, Jay, and Lah worked out together in the mornings. Jah-B got me a job detail in laundry, which I only stayed three hours, 7:30 am to 10:30 am.

USP Atwater is in the middle of nowhere so not too much is going on. The visits were not packed on the weekends and there was no real money being generated on the compound. The food was terrible. They had a very small Unicor factory where they took apart broken computers. That created another hustle... building amplifiers. You could take the computer parts and build an amplifier and make a stereo system to blast your MP3s in your cell. You know I had to get one. I was pretty much laid back but still hated Atwater. I just made the best of it to the best of my ability.

Oceasia was definitely stepping her game back up. She knew I was tired of her disappearances and dropping the ball when I needed her. We spoke once or twice a day but we emailed each other constantly. Inmates could only be on the computers for an hour at a time and we had to wait thirty minutes before we could get back on. The phone had a thirty-minute delay no matter if you only used one minute of the fifteen-minute call. Most of the evenings, I was back and forth from computer to telephone with Oceasia and in no time, was I doing the same with Beauty.

Beauty understood that I had Oceasia and was striving to work things out with her. She gave me all the space in the world and enjoyed my emails and telephone calls. She said she was very grateful for my calls and understood if I didn't call everyday but once I got her local number and a line just for her, she was expecting my calls. They both sent money to the phone account to make sure I could call. Oceasia was my girl, my Earth... the one I truly loved, while Beauty was only a friend.

Lah had just finished reading Love, Hell or Right and was feeling the story. Me, Lah, Jay and Jah-B were hanging out in my cell with the MP3 plugged up to the amplifier and speakers listening to Jay-Z when Lah said...

"Yo, Sha.... my word that love novel is like that. You really surprised me with that. I wasn't expecting a story line like that. You really did your thing."

"Thank you, Lah. I'm glad you enjoyed it" I replied

"I just told my wife to order it and read it. I need her to really understand this struggle like how your Earth understands" Lah said.

"Lah, cut it out Breddren. You got less than three years left and you getting deported. That's the struggle you need to be focusing on" exclaimed Jay as we all laughed.

Lah got married two weeks before I got to Atwater. He married his children's mother, who was also his childhood sweetheart but Jay liked to tease him saying that it was a tactic he pulled so he could stop from being deported. Lah knew that going to Jamaica where he didn't know his family or anybody there would make him feel like a foreigner. He acted like he didn't care about being deported but deep down, he wasn't trying to go.

169

"That's crazy how you can't even chat patios (pa-twah) or nothing Breddren... you a Jamaican that is pure Yankee!" said Jah-B as we laugh on even more.

"Yo, but you're going to amaze a lot of heads back inna yard... for you so Americanized that you got an American accent and all so dem gals dem gon' love you!" Jay reassured as Lah smiled.

"But Lah is married though and he is Muslim" I added. We laughed again.

"True Yankee Bwoy. You and ShaKim Bio... two non-acting Yardies" said Jay.

"Jay... I was born in Brooklyn so don't get that twisted. I was born here" I reminded. "My parents are Yardies... but ShaKim Bio from foreign," I stated as we laughed.

Jay was one of those who spoke with a Brooklyn, New York accent to the fullest but in a split second, he could flip and speak patios with a real heavy Jamaican accent. It was crazy how he did that with ease. I always made jokes about it because he was a Jamaican who repped Brooklyn to the fullest, so much so that if he didn't tell you he was Jamaican, which he didn't off the top, you would never know.

"Yo, Jay... let me ask you something" I spat.

"What's good?" He answered in his Brooklyn talk.

"In yard... they like the rapper 50 Cent?" I asked.

"Yeah, mon... Dem love dat yout in yard... Him big ova there!" Jay exclaimed.

"Word?"

"Yeah... him tear up the whole island when he performed a few years back... dem gals dem love him and gangsters and rudeboys, dem respect him" he added.

"Is that so?" I asked as Lah, Jah-B and Jay looked on.

"Why you ask that?" asked Jay.

"Cause when I get out, I'ma go to the Yard and mash up the island. If they love 50 Cent, they gon' love me. My name is going to be 75 Cents" I said as Lah started laughing.

Jay didn't like that joke at all as Jah-B was shaking his head at me while Lah laughed hysterically at my side jokes at Jay's expense.

While spinning the yard one afternoon, I stopped in the corner where someone had greeting cards lined up on a sheet on the ground. Like I said earlier, there was nothing really going on on the compound that generated money like other Fed pens. Atwater was in the middle of nowhere so you had to get yours by all means. Everything was a hustle. They made and sold handmade apple pies, cheesecakes, frozen ices of all flavors, fruit turnovers, taffy candies, used boots, sneakers... whatever.

Someone had cards that were drawn and whoever drew them definitely had skills. There were cards of all types. They even had sexual exploited ones that used Disney cartoon characters. They were so ill so I bought a few. They came with envelopes ready to go.

I just got off the phone line I reserved for for calling Beauty and she was fresh on my mind when I was writing on one of the cards I'd decided to send to her when Jay and Lah both came to my cell.

"Yo, wha gwaan?" asked Jay as Lah found him a seat in one of my plastic chairs in the cell.

"Writing in this card I'ma shoot out to shorty" I said as I put the card in the envelope.

"Yo, this is a nice ass card" he added as he opened it and saw the inside.

"Bloodclot!... yo, this card wicked Breddren! Your Earth is going to bug out when she opens it. The front throws it off cause you don't expect to see Mickey Mouse putting it on Minnie Mouse like that" We laughed.

The card was ill.

"Yo, that ain't going to my Earth... it's going to the other shorty in Ohio" I said.

"What? You mad or what? Shorty gets this card and she's going to start thinking another way. You don't need to lead her on like so" Jay said.

"Lead her on? Sun, we been talked that talk and the skin out photos been here long time" I revealed.

"Say word God!" he said.

"Word!"

"You dead wrong my dude" Jay said then he and Lah laughed.

"Yo, let me see them joints" said Lah, knowing it was not Muslim-like to see another woman other than his wife in such a manner, especially the photos Beauty sent me.

"Come on Sun. Cut it out. You know it's for my eyes only" I said.

"Yo, I seen regular photos of her, so I know she's holding... that phat ass... ain't it? asked Lah.

"Fall back Ack. I ain't sharing that info" I said sternly but subtle.

"Yo, the Earth is going to shoot you if she finds out" said Lah, chuckling.

"Yeah, Sha... you playing with shorty, knowing your girl loves you" said Jay.

"So now I'm playing games? Yo, Jay, dig Sun. I done penned a novel about the Earth and all that we been

173

through. I put my feelings on paper so the whole world could see and feel my love and shorty goes harder on promoting the novel than my own girl does!" I argued.

"What?" exclaimed Lah.

"Everything that she said she was going to do, she didn't do it yet. She writes for the Five Percenter newspaper. She didn't help me put the ad for my book in there or nothing," I let on.

"That's crazy" barked Lah.

"Bio, why are you still even with her?" asked Jay.

I sat for a few seconds, thinking before I answered...

"Because... I love her." I announced.

"Universal Builders Keep on Building no Matter What"

CHAPTER 19

Reading the Five Percenter newspaper monthly and seeing that attendance at the monthly rallies was decreasing really saddened me. I read about the openings of several Allah youth centers in numerous cities and states to see that months later they ended up closing down due to lack of support.

Reading G. Kalim's editorial as well as Born King and other Gods', such as the Young God "Knowledge Be Allah", and still seeing Earths adding on with their builds still makes my heart smile.

Universal Builders keep on building no matter what. I think back to being in ciphers back in the early, mid and late nineteen eighties. All the Gods who were able to dazzle the crowds with their word play while showing and proving... they made it where you wanted to hear them build [teach]. You were guaranteed to walk away having learned something. They made you want to learn and be smart. I'm talking about Gods who were able to show and prove their lessons to the point that you went and researched where they got those jewels from.

To watch the B.E.T. Hip Hop Awards where they have the freestyle ciphers showed me that many in the young generation do not know where ciphers come from. So many of them don't know that there used to be ciphers in the school yards or on street corners just about everywhere, as Gods stood in a cipher, some were standing in their universal square stance as each brother took turns showing and proving, building on the day's mathematics or lessons. They used to razzle-dazzle the audience with their high explosive builds. Some brothers were known because of their builds (lectures) and how they took control of ciphers.

Universal Builders, always keep on building, no matter what! You don't see that nowadays, especially in these prisons. Real universal builders are the ones, no matter what or where they are, are able and willing to show and prove. I can be anywhere on this Earth and if I am there, Mathematics is there too. Within time, I will have brothers speaking Mathematics... that's how I am. I am a Universal Builder. True and living God. I'm not a sometimes I am God dude. I may not be building on mathematics 24/7 every time you see me but there is never ever a time where I don't or won't know the day's math or won't be able to quote or show and prove. I got brothers who approach me everyday asking me, "What's the mathematics of the day?" brothers who salute me for still carrying on traditions. I still pass the Five Percenter newspaper to other Gods and to brothers who want to read them and when they come back with them, I answer all their questions to the best of my ability. I still go out and build when invited to affairs.

Normally when I touch a new compound, I ask *"where the Gods at?"* I'm used to Gods being everywhere. I grew up in a neighborhood where everyone had K.O.S. (knowledge of self) that was my crowd, my generation. Even when dealing with devilishment and illegal shit, I was around God bodies. Those who didn't have K.O.S. knew the basic math from being in my midst. So when I started asking where the Gods were like in 2005 and beyond and only being directed to two or maybe three brothers on the whole compound where the population was one thousand two hundred and fifty to fifteen hundred convicts. I felt something was terribly wrong and someone was not doing their duty.

Today's prison crowd is mostly the younger generation, coming in with the gang mentality. It isn't cool to have knowledge of self anymore or to be civilized in this crowd. As they get older they then embrace religious faith or absorb some type of knowledge but there are very few, who are absorbing knowledge in their younger years. All they think about is gang banging and gang culture.

I don't knock no one's culture because no matter how one thinks or carries his self, we still ended up in the same place... prison. Now, it's all about bettering one's self and improvement.

So now the Universal Builders are the networkers amongst the prison's population, whom met others from different states, cultures, and nationalities wanting to build relationships to broaden whatever moves they connected on, whether positive or negative.

A Universal Builder is one who can add on in any genre, generation or geographical sphere no matter what. He still does what he does. He is swift and very changeable, knows how to know, look, listen and respect and forever stands on his square. I salute all Universal Builders, Elders, younger generation builders and those in our future generation.

Universal Builders keep on building no matter what!

Loyalty Honor and Respect

"Finding my way back"

Jaheim

CHAPTER 20

Jah-B had me laughing one day, we were building about all kinds of history dealing with women... how they were the cause of the greatest wars in history. We went back to ancient times, to Bible stories to hood stories. It was all the same... women were the cause. He explained how in China, Queens have ruled the entire country. He spoke on the Queen of England who wore thirty-some crowns. He then spoke on female warriors, who challenged male opponents on the battlefield. He spoke on how in most countries, women were put in two categories... housewife and mother and that's it. In several countries, women are power players in corporations or CEO's.

We laughed about tales we shared about our dealings with certain women. I told him how stories of me were circulating in the neighborhood and how when my girl would confront me with stories of me being in the streets or involved in shootouts, I used to be like "Who me?"... nah, Ma, it couldn't be me they spoke on." I told him I didn't let my girl know that about me. Females, who knew about my street dealings, were the ones who were also dealing with street life or caught up in it.

Jah B smiled and said he was like a mouse in front of his girl... a Tiger in front of his enemies. That was Jah-B for you... always reading and sharing the information.

I was constantly arguing with Oceasia. I felt she was being too difficult. Everything that I was asking her to do seemed to be a

180

problem or she just didn't do it. I was asking her to do simple things that required her time. I needed her to look up a few things on the Internet and set up pages for our novel ads to be on. One time I asked that she look into the Allah Youth Center in Dallas, Texas. They had a website that was in the Five Percenter newspaper [the power paper] and she still was writing articles for that paper. This is the same paper that got us together and in tune with each other in the first place.

I wasn't asking her to go out of her way or taking any short cuts. I wanted to earn the benefits of everything I was doing. For one, I was in prison, two, I produced the very first God and Earth love novel in print. So I wanted to work for everything in that sense, born u truth [but] she was acting like she couldn't help me with the simplest things that cost her nothing, only her time. So I was finding others to do the things she couldn't or just wouldn't and I was paying them at that.

Oceasia wanted me to call and email her regularly. If I didn't, she would get upset. I had to explain that even though I'm in prison, I still have things I need to get done. I stay busy. I'm striving to do positive things and get positive results and all her demands and expectations would not help at all.

Beauty on the other hand, was doing so much without me asking. She bought a copy of the novel and had it posted on her FB page, while I had to give Oceasia a copy and she didn't indulge with social media platforms period. So getting her to do anything was hard. I started getting a headache from all her bullshit. I was spending a lot of unnecessary money on promoting and marketing when all I really needed was someone to utilize social media, which is free. I was new to the publishing shit so I was spending money and in return not really making any. I needed help.

I got into an argument with Beauty that woke me up to the reality of her not being my girl. When I received my property from USP Coleman 2, they made me send my beard trimmers home in R&D. Beard trimmers are a commodity as well as a necessity but it was considered contraband in several federal institutions. They used to sell them in commissary but discontinued them due to dudes taking them apart to use the motor to make tattoo guns.

Tattooing can spread hepatitis and HIV, yet it is a common thing in prison. So to slow down or try to stop it, they discontinued selling beard trimmers but if you had a pair, you were allowed to keep them. You just couldn't transfer to another facility with them. So the price of them was tripled due to their importance.

I kept my head shaved bald. I couldn't use a razor so I had to use beard trimmers or hair clippers. Beard trimmers are the closest thing to hair clippers. I needed beard trimmers, no question. Atwater, being a spot that generates no money, has no real economy so everything is overpriced for others to survive. I went to the barbershop to get a haircut and facial shape up. My hair was practically so low that it was stubble, if that. I like to get my head shaved every three or four days. The barber quoted me a price that made me think he was on drugs. He just couldn't have been serious. No way!

It so happened that I was in the unit early one morning - just getting off the computer when this convict came up to me and asked if I was interested in buying some beard trimmers. I was like *"what?"* I asked to see them and he took them out of his pocket. They had brand new batteries in them. I had to ask him if they were stolen and he told me he had two pairs and decided to sell one. After trying out the trimmers I asked the price and he gave me a nice price. I took his info and told him that I would get the money sent within two hours.

I couldn't catch anyone on the phone to have send the money. I needed the money sent to his account right away.

It was an early Sunday morning so I called Beauty. She answered and accepted the call. We spoke for a minute or two and I asked her if she could spare one hundred and ten dollars [$100 to send to dude's account, $10 to send it Western Union]. She said yes and I gave her the info. She said she would take care of it as soon as our call was over. She took care of that and I got the trimmers and everything was everything.

Later on that night, I called one of my street comrades, gave him Beauty's number and told him to call and get her info so he could send her the money back.

A few days later she emailed me asking me to call her and that it was important. I called later that night. She asked why did I send her the money back. I explained that I really needed the trimmers and couldn't catch anyone that early on a Sunday so I asked her but I didn't want to take away from her, knowing she had bills and expenses. She told me that she didn't respect that and explained how she was willing to go all out for her man and I should accept that. She did that for me and it wasn't for me to give her the money back.

We argued about that. I told her that I understood where she stood but she had to understand something. She wasn't my girl... Oceasia D. True Earth was my girl. That put her in her place.

Then she asked why I call her so often or email her regularly. Why does she do more for my novel than Oceasia if Oceasia is my girl? She wanted to know why I had a whole three hundred minutes reserved for calling her if Oceasia was my girl? Why did I send her those sexual cards if Oceasia was my girl? Why the daily emails if Oceasia was my girl? She was acting like she didn't know from the beginning that Oceasia was my girl. Then she asked me "Are you sure Oceasia is your girl? ... because she sure don't act like it. If she did, you wouldn't be on the phone with me." She told me to get back at her once I decided what I'm going to do with her and my girl.

As I hung up the phone and went to my cell, turned on my amp and radio. Jaheim's song, I thought back to what Ike told me in the box when we were cellies in Coleman. "Finding my way back" came on the radio and that made me realize what I needed to do. That's all I needed to hear.

"These lips… can't wait to taste your skin

and these eyes can't wait to see your grin"

"Adorn"

Miguel

CHAPTER 21

March 1st through 3rd of 2013, Oceasia flew out to USP Atwater to come see me for the weekend. It was a visit that was very well needed. I needed to know where she stood and what future she was building for us. I got objectives and goals that I am aiming to accomplish and I don't need any one holding me back. I needed to be assured that I wasn't playing myself and opening myself up to get hurt again. She also said that she had a surprise for me.

The visiting set up was much differently in Atwater. We could hug and kiss in the beginning of the visit and at the conclusion of the visit. We sat across from each other. We weren't allowed to touch or hold hands, even though I found ways to touch her anyway. We did get to take photos in which we fondled each other like little misbehaving school kids.

When I came out to the visit looking like the Don that I am, her eyes lit up as she ran into my arms. We kissed like no tomorrow as I squeezed her into me and breathed in her scent. After about five minutes of our foreplay, we sat down across from each other.

"Bay... what are you doing in here? Look at your arms... they're so big!" she observed while reaching to squeeze my arms. Of course, we were reminded and warned not to touch each other, by the C.O.

"This isn't the only thing big on me either" I joked.

Oceasia had her hair cut short... It was jazzy. She had it faded on the sides with designs lined in with "The Illest" drawn in on one side. She was killing her "Kelis" look. She had on some skinny jeans and a dark blue tight-fitting sweatshirt with a photo of Young Evher Peace holding up the novel of "Love, Hell or Right" on the front. She was rocking some laced up boots that most chicks were styling in the free cipher. Oceasia was still looking good as she sat there beaming her smile at me.

I sat there smiling back. I was in my neatly ironed beige prison-issued khaki pants and shirt, rocking my baldhead, mustache and facial hair was all crispy lined up with my brand new black Timberland boots.

"I see that you are repping our novel well" I stated then I complimented her. "You're definitely looking good."

"I'm repping us Bae... it's sometimes you... sometimes me.... Always us and never them... Why?... You forgot?" she asked as she raised an eyebrow.

"How could I ever forget?" I replied as I thought back to all the good and not so good memories we created and shared together within our 9-year relationship, where we were never physically intimate but on we were intimate on every other level were.

"You smelling all so good, Bae... what is that you are wearing because it's not Egyptian musk" she asked.

"Nah... they got a new fragrance oil here called "Jay-Z" I enlightened her.

"For real? It smells really good" she responded.

We spoke about her family... then we spoke on mine. I still loved Oceasia and the love was still apparent but I was striving to make moves that made differences and generated currency. I wanted to build a future and legacy... something productive and positive. I wanted to build all this with her included but I wanted to be sure that she wanted the same. We were straying away a bit [maybe more] but I couldn't lose my focus. I knew what direction I wanted to go in. So this visit was very much needed. I needed to know where we stood... where she stood. I had given her an ultimatum... she was either rocking with me or she wasn't.

The first day of our visit... Everything was all love. We started out joking and playing. We got the cards, then the checkers... we were having fun. About four hours into the visit I asked her "Ma... where you at? Where do you stand? Where do we stand?"

"I'm here... ain't I?" was her response as we locked eyes.

From there the conversation as well as the temperature in the visiting room got HEATED. We went back and forth, she kept on and on about knowing deep down that there were other females in my life... that I was up to something. She was getting loud and carried away as I let her vent. She even started pointing her fingers towards me. Then she came across the so called table and started jabbing her fingers in my face, telling me I better not be playing no games with her or her feelings. She got real emotional as tears started streaming down her face. Of course, I was looking like the bad guy in the visiting room and everyone started looking in our direction. Some of the female visitors were shaking their heads and giving me disgusted looks. The C.O.

188

came over to us twice, to tell us [really her] to quiet down... I just sat there, taking her finger pointing in my face, screaming on me and all that other drama. I put my head down in my lap and guess what she did? She plucked me in my head [hard too]. "Wow!" I stated as I looked at her deep into her eyes.

"So to clean up the bullshit you doing out there... you come in here and put the blame on me? I'm the bad guy and you goody two-shoes? You're worrying about other females?" I asked her. "If you feel I'm playing with you and your feelings... then go... why stay?" I stated as I pointed to the door. "Go ahead and go... leave and don't ever come back" I quietly barked with venom as I stared in her teary eyes.

"Go ahead and leave," I repeated.

"That's what you want me to do?" she asked.

"If that's what you want... then go." I responded.

As Oceasia sat there staring at me... studying me... who knows what was going on in her mental, what she was seeing and thinking... whatever it was, she didn't leave.

"Now I'm going to ask you again... where do you stand?" I asked as I straightened up in my seat preparing myself for her answer. She knew I was sick and tired of playing games with her and was ready to move on without her.

She pointed at me and answered.

"I stand with you... always and forever."

189

We sat there, staring in each other's eyes… minutes passed by without one word being said. Then I broke the silence.

"Go to the bathroom and wash your face then come back and tell me an Evher Peace story."

She smiled and rose from her seat to please her God.

The remainder of the visit for that day was good. We enjoyed each other's company and spoke about me giving time back to the government a second time and all the excitement surrounding my upcoming novel [the 2nd one], to us and all about us. She was telling me about how fast Evher was growing and how smart she was. Evher was upset that she didn't come to see me. She wanted to see me bad, too. She was now writing rhymes and promising to spit something exclusive just for me but she always got shy when I asked her too. We laughed together at the Evher Peace stories. Evher called herself "The Illest Evher" something that she adopted from me, of course.

"Bae?"

"What's good my BBD," I asked.

That right there just put a big smile on Oceasia's face… still being called by my "BBD." I gave her that title in 2004. BBD… beautiful breathing diamond.

"I got this song I want you to get on your MP3… it's two songs," she said.

"Ok. What are they?" I asked.

"You going to get them?" She asked putting a question on top of my question. She'd been giving me a list of songs to get so my MP3 had a playlist of songs that I got just for her.

"Get these two songs, Bae - "4 Ever" by Lil Mo and get "Stay Together" by Ledisi, featuring Jaheim.

"I already have Lil Mo's song" I answered.

"Ok but get Ledisi's song" she said.

"I will do it tonight."

"Don't call me until you get it and listen to both of them," she stated as she pointed her finger at me.

"I know you better keep your finger in check and stop playing," I said as I warned her and we both burst out laughing.

"9-12-21 ShaKim," she said.

"9-12-21 Oceasia," I answered back.

"You better," she said.

The next morning I was up and ready as soon as the doors were opened at 5:47am. I went and got in my regular hard body workout, which lasted about fifty minutes to an hour. Then, I went and had Jay, who was now my celly, go over my already crispy bald head with the trimmers and lined my facials, which didn't need it. It was all about being on point and fresh to death especially for dance floor events [prison visits].

We, men, go all out to make sure we are looking good. We got to have every little detail in place and on point. Once I was satisfied that everything was good, as soon as they made the breakfast call, I made the move just to link up with my NY comrades and Jamaican massive. After the back and forth walking up and down the walkway conversing and building with fellow convicts, I made it back to the unit to call my Earth, Oceasia, to make sure she was up and everything was good.

I put her to sleep last night as we burned like over one hundred minutes on several phone lines with our back and forth love vows and her thirty plus minutes of 'phone love' which was amazing. I dialed her number and put my nine pac digit in with the quickness and did the voice matching. After four rings... I heard her pick up.

"Hello?"

"This call is from a federal prison, this is a prepaid call. You will not be charged for this call. This call is from ShaKim Bio... hang up if you want to decline the call. If you want to accept this call, press 5. To block any future calls from this inmate, press 7."

She pressed '5' and said

"Peace, Bae."

"Peace BBD! Just making sure you're up and getting ready."

"You know I'ma be up to see you, Bae. I'm crazy about you... that's why I still put up with your shit!" she joked but I knew somehow, in her mind, she really felt she was putting up form of mistreatment or wrong doing on my part.

"Yeah? Is that so?" I asked with a sarcastic tone.

"You know I gotta really love you God, to be going through all this with a man in prison, who I met in prison. I really and truly love you ShaKim. We are soul mates forever."

"Forever... ever, Ma?" I asked her.

"Forever... ever, Bae. Wait until I get back up there in an hour. I gotta show you what my surprise is."

"Yeah... true indeed... I been waiting on this surprise"

I took a nice hot shower and got ready for my visit with Oceasia. I had my khaki shirt hanging on a hanger, which I was taking up to the visiting room's dressing area to put on before I stepped into the V.I. room.

I rubbed some Kush fragrance oil but just a few drops applied to the right spots so I wouldn't overdo it but at the same time, it wouldn't go unnoticed. I was lacing up my black Timbs when the C.O. came to my door and told me that I had a visit. I grabbed my hanger with my crispy shirt, made sure I had my photo tickets and ID and made my way to the visiting hall.

"Yo, ShaKim Bio... have a good visit Rudebwoy," Jay said as I passed him and the crew playing dominoes at the table by the unit's door.

"No doubt"

I got to the visiting room dressing area... got logged in, got fully dressed and looked in the mirror. I even brought my toothbrush and toothpaste to brush my teeth and tongue making sure everything was on point. I also had some candy to sweeten up my breath and tongue so when we kissed, I tasted good too. Yeah... everything and I mean everything had to be right and exact... and on point.

I stepped into the visiting hall and saw Oceasia sitting there in the second row. There weren't many other people in there. One thing about USP Atwater, their visiting room was never packed. There were about four other convicts with their loved ones and families. If there were anywhere close to fifteen convicts with their families in there it would have been considered "packed". That's how bad it was visiting that institution.

As I walked to her, Oceasia raised up and opened her arms, ready for me to step into her world and space.

"Peace, Bae" she said as she wrapped her arms around my neck.

We kissed passionately and I massaged her lower back, my hands making my way down to squeeze something round and soft. "Mmmmm" was her response as we deeply inhaled each other's scent and enjoyed our intimate moment. A lot of convicts make comments about passionately kissing or even kissing their female or any female on visits.

Popular prison consensus says being locked up while your woman or female friend is out there in the free world, there's no telling what she's been doing or who she's been doing it with. You remember the nasty things y'all did together and you can't imagine what she is doing nowadays so you don't kiss at all on that level.

I understand... but me? I don't kiss any female like that either but when it comes to someone who I love and care about? I'ma kiss the life out of her. I don't think about what she might be doing... the visits be all about us and what we are doing. I love women and being around women. I appreciate everything about them so when she finds time to make time to travel long distance to come check my pulse after everyone else gave up on me or isn't checking for me like that, you know I'm going to spoil her and make those visiting days all about her. I'ma kiss her, tongue her and suck on her lips... that's just me. I sucks on her neck... let my hands roam and get my squeezes and feels on. She is going to love that about me... but moving along...

"Damn, Bae... I love the way you kiss me. It's like you making love to my lips" Oceasia proclaimed.

She came closer for another one and as I leaned in to plant it on her, she stopped me so she could suck on my bottom lip. I stepped back to check her out and absorb her beauty. Oceasia was / is so beautiful in my eyes. She was rocking an all black tight jean suit with those black lace mid heel boots that made her taller than the five feet two inches she stood naturally and again, she was killing that low Kelis hairstyle.

"You smelling good" she said, smiling like a little girl and looking just like her daughter, Evher Peace.

I smiled back and checked out her earrings. She wore some small box radio joints; the kind of box radio that my generation used to roll in the park with, pumping cassette tapes; the kind that a lot of dudes were robbed, beat down and sometimes shot and killed for. She was definitely on her ol' school shit to be six years younger than me. She was still an emcee true to heart.

"Damn, Ma.... those earrings are ill. Where you get them from?" I asked as I sat down in my chair in front of her. My eyes were on the same level where her crotch area was.

"I ordered them online from this hip hop site. They cute, right?" She asked, laughing now as she noticed what my eyes were glued to.

"Bae... you better stop before you start something you can't finish." She warned.

She acted like she was going to come to me and put her leg in my chair, standing in front of me so she would be opened legged with coochie in my face. We laughed and were clowning around but I wished it could have really happened.

As she took off her jean jacket, I saw that she was wearing an official RUN DMC t-shirt. I mean, it was the straight up official joint. She stood in her B-girl stance, showing off and being goofy for me.

I noticed that my Earth was really tatted up. I looked at her and briefly studied her unique artwork. As she took her seat across from me, I noticed something on her arm.

"Oceasia, let me see your arm, Ma" I said.

"Why?" smiling, she sassed, knowing what I had seen.

"Nah… for real… let me see your arm" I repeated.

She tried to give me her other arm.

"Stop playing, let me see your other arm!" I said, reaching for her arm, knowing that we weren't allowed to touch one another once we were seated.

She smiled as she lifted her arm up so I could study the tattoo on her forearm. It was my signature, the same exact way I sign my name.

"When did you get that?" I asked in surprise and wonder.

"A few days ago," she replied with a huge smile on her face.

"How did the tattoo artist get my name to look like I did it?"

"Easy... I took one of the Valentine's Day cards you sent and had him lift your signature off of it to make the pattern. You like it?"

"Nah... I love it." I replied with excitement.

I rubbed her skin, again, knowing I was violating and running the risk of having our visit terminated for touching.

"I love you so much, I needed your signature all over me" she said.

"Is that so... how is my name all over you?"

She put her left hand out to show me her wedding ring finger, which had my name inked on it, vertically. It said ShaKim Bio and again it was my signature she had lifted off of a letter I sent her. I was very impressed by how my Earth Oceasia was repping me like that.

"Yeah... I know you see it. Mr. ShaKim Bio... I am all yours. I put it where everybody will be able to see it. Everybody knows that I love you" she announced.

"I love you too" I confirmed.

"I wasn't going to let no New York City slicker outdo a country girl like me by getting my name tatted on his hand. I had to outdo you, Bae" she said.

Oceasia smiled her little girl smile and laughed her little cute laugh. I raised my right hand up so she could view her name tattooed on me.

"Sha... I miss holding that hand and kissing and licking that tattoo" she said as she put her upset face game on.

"I miss it too, Oceasia. I truly appreciate and cherish you for a long list of reasons"

"I believe you too, Bae."

"I wish I could walk out of here with you right now" I said, sadly.

"Where will we go?" she asked.

"First stop... back to your hotel room so I can put in that work!" I made sure that that was known as fact.

"I wish I could climb in your lap so we could set it off right now" she said as we stared into each other's eyes, in our world of love.

CHAPTER 22

I was walking back to my unit after that lovely visit. I had to get back to the realization that I was in a concrete and steel jungle full of men with animal characteristics; some of them, wild animals that prey on anything and some that was straight up harmless and in the way to the point that they were in everybody's way. Nevertheless, prison is a very dangerous ground because a lot of convicts are amongst the walking dead.... dead mentally but not physically.

Oceasia and I had a ball in that visiting room. We took all kinds of photos. She had me doing old school poses and all. We were really clowning. I only did that because of her official RUN-DMC throwback t-shirt plus I could let my guard down and be a kid around her.

I couldn't wait to call her later that night and re-live the great time we just had. We took photos of us hugging, holding hands, and she made sure to let that tattoo of my name on her forearm be seen as much as possible. We had so much fun. She told me that she was going to find a way to come and see me more often. For the conversations, to our little love quarrels, to playing cards and checkers [I even let her win a few times], our visits were lovely and we had a ball. We had one visit left on this weekend trip and I was going to make sure it was just as lovely.

"How was the "V" Sun?" asked one of my comrades from the east coast.

"Shit was love-love... I really enjoyed myself" I responded.

"Was it packed out there?" He asked.

"What?" It was like maybe 10 heads out there including families, if that. You know ain't nobody coming way out here in the middle of nowhere to see someone" I said.

"Shit... someone came to see you" he joked."Who came up?"

"Wifey," I said.

"No doubt God... that Love, Hell or Right was the truth" he said as he gave me a pound handshake.

I was lying up on my bunk, thinking and listening to music on my MP3 player. I went to my playlist where I kept my slow jams. As I listened to Mint Condition, reflected on the visit I just had with Oceasia. I listened to the lead singer, Stokely, croon about how that particular female kept him swinging "Girl you send me swingin'...'". I pressed the rewind button to restart the song.

5:45am the next morning, I was back at it again. I was getting my workout on. I had to stop at 6:15 because I promised Oceasia I would give her a wake up call and see what's good with my beautiful breathing diamond.

After the recording, she pressed '5' and I greeted her...

"What's good BBD?"

"You... it's 6:15. You were supposed to call at 6am mister always on point" she said sarcastically.

"Yeah, Ma. I know. I was working out and got carried away. You know this is the time I usually workout but I cut it short to make time for you" I reminded.

"You better. I'm wifey" she quipped.

"True indeed."

"I can't wait until this whole prison ordeal is finally over so I can have you all to myself... waking up to you every morning... cooking... raising a family... stuff that couples in love do. I need you here ShaKim... I really want you home with me where you are supposed to be" she said.

"I think about that aspect more than anything, Ma. Nobody wants me home more than I do. Believe me, I'm the one doing this time" I said, thinking about it more.

"No, you're not. You ain't the only one doing this time. It's like I'm doing this time with you... I'm here ain't I?" she asked with an attitude.

"We will finish this conversation when you get up here"

I wasn't in the mood to be going back and forth.

"Ok, I'ma be sure to bring it up too"

I guess she was giving me a heads up.

"Ok, make sure you do that. Anyway, let me get back to my workout and get myself in order so I'm ready when they call me."

"Stop it, Sha... you know you're going to be ready way before that!" she said in a joking manner to lighten up the mood. She knew I was getting upset.

"I'll be ready... make sure you are"

"I love you, Bae."

"Love you too"

We hung up.

After completing my work out of twenty sets of pull ups, push ups, dips, and some arm curls with the 40 pound sand bags, I got my celly, Jay, to go back over my bald head with the trimmers and line me up. Believe me, a little stubble was there... unless it was dead skin. I had to make sure that I was on point all across the board. I had my visiting gear ironed earlier within the week. I skipped out on going on the walkway to chop it up with my comrades during the breakfast call.

I sat in the cell and meditated, getting my thoughts together. I had been gone over nineteen going on twenty years already... that's two decades. A lot of things changed within the world from the way people lived, technology, to the newer generation. Just about everything changed and I was still in prison. That bothered me a lot like I know it bothers every man or woman in prison. To think about their time... and to think not many convicts doing their time have loved ones to reach out to them. Some don't experience visits. I'm fortunate to still have family and loved ones that check up on me. I was truly blessed to have Oceasia. I truly appreciated, cherished and loved that woman. As I was in another world caught up in my thoughts, I snapped out of it and looked at my watch. It was time for me to shower and get ready to see my Earth.

My name was called as I got my picture tickets, I.D. and clothes hanger with my khaki shirt on it and made my way towards the door. I gave a head nod to my celly as I went out the door, he smiled and shouted as the door closed

"Shine out there God!"

I made it up to the v.i. room in lightning speed, I got logged in, changed into my khaki shirt and went to the mirror to make sure everything was everything. Like the past two previous days, I was one of the first ones in the visiting room. Oceasia wasn't playing no games. We needed every second of every minute of every hour we had to visit each other... Fuck that!

I made it out to the visiting room to the officer's post to hand in my I.D. Oceasia was sitting in the same row, same seat as yesterday like she never left. We made eye contact and she waved at me smiling. I started smiling as well. She stood up as I made my way to her. She had on the "Love, Hell or Right" sweatshirt again with another pair of tight jeans and she switched up the foot -gear too. She was rocking some silver looking thick-soled mid-high sneakers. She was watching me look at her feet and opened her arms to greet me as I approached her.

"Peace, Bae!" she said as we embraced.

I squeezed her tightly around her body as her arms were around my neck. Our lips met and we kissed passionately like there was no tomorrow. I smelled her perfume and I could taste the sweetness of the candy she must have recently eaten. My hands ran down her back to her small phat ass and they squeezed, they squeezed, not me... it was them, the hands LOL. Wishing I could make my way between her legs but we were in the same aisle the C.O. was posted in so I couldn't try my hand yet... but I was planning to do it at the end of the visit. This was our last day. She stopped kissing me to suck on my bottom lip.

"Oooh, Bae... I love kissing you... You are so passionate and a great kisser... Your lips are like that" she said as she went in for another kiss.

Oceasia is five feet, two inches tall and I'm five - ten. Those eight inches make a difference because I had to hunch my back as she stands on her toes to meet me. This time, I wrapped my arms around her small waist and lifted her up to me. She giggled. We were really clowning as I put her back down and squeezed her again. I love that girl. I relished in thought as I took my seat across from her.

"I saw the way you were peeping me... what? You don't like my tennis shoes?" she asked, as she crossed her legs and put her foot in her lap.

"It's cool, Ma... I was just peeping you... that's all" I responded.

"What was on your mental when you were peeping me" Oceasia asked.

"A lot of things... I was looking at how tight those jeans are fitting you. Evher really did a lot of justice to you cause now you got a nice little fatty back there" I said playfully.

"I know... I need to lose some weight" she said.

"Nah, Ma... you good... just like that" I assured her.

"What else were you thinking about?" she asked.

I laughed.

"You think you know me so damn well... huh?"

She smiling at my question.

"I was thinking about how you got knowledge of self... knowing 120 and you don't be living out your culture or be showing and proving. You wearing tight ass jeans... When am I ever going to see you covered in three-fourths?" I inquired.

"I came up here to see you and I came to look good for you. I came to see you before wearing a dress... so stop it. I still know 120 but I'm not showing and proving no more.

I'm being a single mother to Evher and a wife to you... that's what's important to me right now. We got all the time in the world to get us together as far as showing and proving to the world... Right now, it's about me showing and proving to you and you showing and proving to me"

She was serious, looking into my eyes the whole time she spoke.

"I love you, Bae and I want to do whatever you want and need me to do... I told you that I stand with you" she said, pointing her finger at me.

"I hear you, Ma"

"I know you hear me but I need you to feel and overstand me ShaKim."

That right there brought a big smile across my face.

While drinking some orange juice and getting my eat on with some spicy chicken wings, I looked at Oceasia. She was smiling and just watching me eat.

"Ma... you hip to this singer named Raheem DeVaughn?" I asked.

"Yeah, I heard of him... he got some nice songs out" she said.

"This morning while working out, I had his song 'Woman' on repeat on my MP3 player" I said to her.

"Yeah, You like that song, huh?"

"Yeah… I'm really feeling that joint. If I knew how to sing, I would sing that song to you because the lyrics are so on point." I said, still thinking about the song.

"Oh, word? ShaKim would sing that song to me? I'm overwhelmed to hear that" she said while trying to hold back her smile.

"But I'm serious though Tamekia,"

I called her by her government name, a name that no one uses, not even her mother. I'm the only one who can do that and it really catches her attention.

"I appreciate you and everything you've done for me and that song really expresses that."

"Ok… sing it to me then" she challenged.

"I said IF I knew how to sing"

We both bust out laughing.

"I still love you even more if you didn't know how to sing"

"You better"

After enjoying games of checkers and cards, we were laughing and reliving some Evher Peace stories. Oceasia told me how fast young Evher was growing up and learning, she looked at me and said.

"ShaKim... let me ask you this because what I know about you and see in you is not the same that is said about you. You know people read about you in the papers on the Internet... I know you... What are you going to do once you make it out of prison? What's on your agenda?"

Oceasia sat up to absorb my answer. I looked at her and thought deeply because I have several plans but not one in particular I could say is THEE one.

"I want to write some screenplays, maybe have them produced as a feature film but I want to write. I trust that these these novels will do a little something, if not, I'ma keep writing and striving. I'm also absorbing information about medical supplies and medical transportation. I need to do more research on that because I'ma need money and proposals for grants to get that done. I'm also looking into cleaning solar energy panels. I'm reading that that's a good move. Those are my long-term goals but when I touch [get out], I'ma reach out to my so-called associates in the industry and see if I can get a gig to get me by. Whatever I do, believe me I'm not going back to selling drugs or any street activity that involves illegal shit."

That made Oceasia smile.

"I've got to get on point with technology and how to work with this computer shit. I know everything is online and computerized nowadays. I took a Microsoft computer class but it wasn't really hands on like that. Just the basic shit" I explained.

I had her full attention. I've taken advantage of a lot of programs since I've been in prison. I obtained my G.E.D. and got a lot of courses under my belt. I just completed a small business class. She knew that I was no slouch or lame ass cat who only depends on illegal activity. I have a great entrepreneurial spirit.

"What's up with these other chicks you got?"

She came from out of nowhere with that question.

"What?"

"Stop the bullshit...don't sit there like you ain't been in touch with Tammi and whoever else... I read the novel."

"Oh, you read the book, huh?"

"Yeah... it made me cry... laugh... it made me angry... it was a very emotional book and it was also very special to me. I didn't dig a few things you said but I understood. Overall, I loved it so never get that wrong"

"Yeah?"

Honestly, I was happy to finally hear her talk about the book itself and how she felt about it because I wrote and it was about us... I thought I'd never hear anything about it from her.

"What I didn't appreciate was how you described Tammi, like she was all of that, like she was some superstar runway model but you got me sounding like all plain and regular. Yeah, I didn't dig that"

I started laughing.

"That shit ain't funny!" she griped, hitting me on my leg.

"Yeah... but look who won the God and has me all to herself"

"How about this other chick, Robin?" she inquired.

"What about her? I don't even know shorty... I haven't spoken to her since that visit."

"Where's Tammi, y'all still in touch?" she asked.

"Nah... I haven't heard from Tammi in a while. Since like 2008 I think. I asked her to write a letter to the judge for me on the first motion I won. A lot of people did one for me. Daymond John of FUBU, a few friends and family... She hit me back on some "let that country chick you chose over me do it" type shit"

I locked my eyes in Oceasia's, dead serious, because not only did Tammi not come through with the letter to the courts on my behalf... Oceasia didn't either. She looked down to the floor on that note.

"What about these other chicks? I know you got them"

"Why you so worried about other chicks? If you'd been playing your position and doing what you're supposed to be doing, there wouldn't be any room for the next chick. It

211

ain't like I'm with the next chick sitting on visits or planning a future or some shit. These are the chicks who are making sure that my shit is getting done... helping me promote, market and push the novel I wrote about YOU. You ain't doing nothing... so don't question me about no other chick"

"So you going to sit here and admit that you're dealing with other chicks? You need to dead all that shit now because when you come home with that bullshit, I'ma shoot you and her... and I'm not playing!"

She put her serious game face on, daring me to test her. I sat there with a smirk on my face.

"You think I'm playing don't you?" she asked.

"I don't know" I replied knowing when I do that... that it pisses her off.

"I know now that you don't love me... You sitting there with a smirk on your face, knowing you want to laugh in my face at my demands of wanting YOU... all to myself. You just admitted that you are dealing with other chicks... next thing you know, they're going to be visiting you. You hugging and kissing... and when you get out... you'll be going to fuck them... you sitting there thinking that's how it's going be, huh? You can't possibly love me like you claim."

I could see in her face, she was PISSED.

"You don't really love me... Do you ShaKim?... Go ahead and tell me. Tell me that you don't really love me" she demanded.

She looked as if she were about to "lose it" in the visiting room.

Looking at her, I blanked out for sixty seconds and what came to mind was Beauty's phone conversation on how I needed someone who really appreciated and cherished me; someone who would have my back all the way until the end. She claimed I deserved more and could do way better. She knew I loved Oceasia and she respected me for that but was Oceasia really going to be there? Does she love me like she claims? What is my worth to her?

I thought about the Earth, My "Precious Queen" from South Carolina, who told me that I talked about Oceasia so much that she knew she must love me and represent me fully. I thought about all the females that were in my life from before I was incarcerated to all these years I'd been locked up. I thought of both my son's mothers... all of the women just flashed in my mind at a great terrific speed, it was like I saw through the penitentiary walls... through the concrete and steel.

Oceasia stared at me, seeing how I was clearly lost in deep thought.

"ShaKim... I'm waiting on you to tell me the truth"

Her voice snapped me out of my deep daze and brought me back into reality.

213

"Let me ask you this question, Tamekia... How many men do you know or have you even heard about, who sit down and write a book about their girl and it's close to four hundred pages? ... and you ask me if I love you? Stop fuckin' playin' with me" I warned her.

She sat there with nothing to say because the truth had been spoken.

We took like ten to fifteen photos. We were having a ball and at the same time getting our feels and grind on. Oceasia kept slipping her hand in my pants to get a feel of the iron. She was really enjoying herself but leaving me in a messed up position to walk back to our seating area.

She wanted to take a photo of us kissing so she had to find an ill position, which she did by standing in front of me holding hands with our hands intertwined and arms extended, then she raised her head to kiss me. We took another one like that but instead of having our arms extended, mine was wrapped in front of her with our hands still intertwined. It was a beautiful photo. We got a chance to view each photo to see each photo after they were taken because of the high definition, digital camera. We argued who was going to keep which one but she wanted all of them. I told her I wasn't sending her all of them for her to make copies because the last time I did that she kept most of them and sent me what she wanted me to have. So I told her I was going to get the copies made first then send her copies for her to keep. She was whining but it was all love.

As we were slow walking back to our seating area, Oceasia stopped and grabbed my hand and said...

"Bae".

"What's good, Ma?"

"You know that you shut me up when you asked what man have I ever known to pen his love for his woman. I couldn't answer that or say anything... you got that... I know you love me. I just don't want to lose you or share you with anyone. I want you to be all mine. I know when another woman is tryna take what's mine. I have radar for that.... Tell her to step... do that for me"

I held her hand and kept walking to our seats. I didn't respond. I just squeezed her hand into mine tighter.

"No matter what... wherever you go, I'ma look for you and find you. I'ma follow you to the end of the earth. You are mine. I know I sometimes fall short and you may deserve better but I'm really, really trying. It's hard loving a man in prison but I'm always and forever going to be there. I'm with you all the way until the end. Even when you're not going to want me no more. I'm going to still want you, Bae. I love you ShaKim Bio. Please know and understand that. It's always us." She said looking directly at me.

I stopped in front of my seat and faced her.

"I promise you, Bae. It's always US" she said again.

I wanted to believe her and as I looked down at her... she was smiling at me... deep down, I knew she loved me. I knew she really did. I just didn't want to be hurt again. I smiled at her and I said

"Just remember everything you said to me from March first through today, March third 2013. The purpose of this visit was to tell me and reassure me where we stood and where you stand. I just want you to know that your word is your bond regardless to whom or what."

"Yes, Bae... my word is bond... I'm with you" she reassured.

*   *   *

We closed the visit at the very end. As soon as the C.O. gave the visiting room the warning that visits would be coming to a close in five minutes, I stood up. I wanted to get those five minutes in and go beyond that, which added maybe another three or so minutes. I pulled Oceasia into me and wrapped my arms around her tightly.

"Thank you so much for coming up to see me, Ma. I really needed to see you. This visit meant a lot to me" I stressed.

As she squeezed me back, she whispered..

"I need you ShaKim... I need you with me... I need you home."

We looked at each other as she came up to reach my mouth and we made music with our lips and tongues that I titled 'Sweet, Wet, and Passionate'.

The ill thing about a visit is the ending part... that is the most emotional part for both parties because your loved one is heading out the door to freedom and you're still stuck in the harsh reality of hell. They keep looking back, waving and you're waving... You're wishing you could leave with them but you know that you can't... They say "Bye" with tears in their eyes. You're wondering if you will ever see them again and thinking how you really enjoyed their company.

Seeing my Oceasia leave took a lot out of me.   I wanted to leave with her. Something told me that my heart went out that door with her too and it will never ever be the same.

"Song Cry"

Jay-Z

CHAPTER 23

I was sitting on the blue steel picnic table that was in the far corner of the trackside of the rec yard. King Jahzerah Allah Mathematics, also known as "Hoffa" and I were going through some lessons and just speaking on things in general. The God was telling me about his ordeal, how he was in Tennessee doing his thing and ended up with two life sentences. I was asking him if any of the new federal drug amendments would help him. Shit is crazy how brothers get life for selling drugs and no violence or murder is involved.

"Yo, Hoffa… word life these drug laws are ill. They be giving us so much time for drugs that don't involve no bodies. No violence, none of that. Brothers be getting oiled up and given football numbers or letters to do."

"I know"

"Selling drugs is not even worth all the risks no more for all the fake luxury living and all that. All of that is gone and they still want their time out of us.

"Tell me about it Sha. I got two life sentences" said Hoffa.

"On the bricks, we knew nothing about these conspiracy laws and how they can give us time with no physical evidence, drugs or anything… just circumstantial and hear-say can do… this is us." I thought aloud.

"Word, Sha… The equality degree in the knowledge - knowledge culture [6th degree in the 1-14, which is lost and

219

found Muslim lesson #1] states: Why does the devil teach and keep our people illiterate?

"What's the answer Sha?" He asked me.

"Answer... so that he can use them as a tool and also a slave. He keeps them blind to themselves so that he could master them. Illiterate means ignorant." I answered.

"That's how it is... we are caught up in the fake illusion of that reality in our environment" said Hoffa.

"Hmmmm."

"ShaKim... take the word "tool" and the word "slave" and born them out" he requested.

"Huh?"

"Born them out for me. The word "tool" and the word "slave.""

"Tool is 20, 15, 15, 12, that's 35 plus 27.. that's 62," I responded.

"What's that all being born too?" He asked.

"To build or destroy," I said.

"Now, do "slave"

"19, 12, 1, 22, 5, which equals 59, which equals 14," I spit.

"All being born to what?" He asked.

"Power"

"Put tool which born Build and slave which Born power. Put those two words together." He directed.

"Build power" I finished before he could.

"Yeah... the eighty-five percent of the population, which the devil teaches and keeps illiterate" added Hoffa.

"That's an ill way to show and prove that mathematically," I said, laughing.

"Yeah... Mathematics is ill like that. That's why I love Supreme Mathematics!" shouted Hoffa.

Later on that night, while I was sitting in my cell thinking about life itself and where I stood, I thought about the Loyalty, Honor and Respect that I am so in need of.

Loyalty is the state of quality of being loyal, faithful to, commitments or obligations, devotion, fidelity, all imply a sense of duty or of devoted attachment to something or someone. Loyalty "borned" knowledge-knowledge cipher [110] all being born to wisdom [2]

Honor is integritry in one's belief and actions, high respect, as for worth, merit such respect manifested. Honor "borned" God Cipher [70] all being born to God [7]

Respect is esteem for or a sense of the worth or the excellence of a person, a personal quality or ability or something considered as a manifestation of a person's quality or ability, the conditions of being esteemed or honored. Respect "borned" Build equality [86] "borning" knowledge culture [14] all being born to Power [5]

I took the definitions and then took what they borned out to and applied them to the science of mathematics and the everyday reality of life, my reality, and stood up, left my cell on my way to the telephones to call two females on the separate phone lines I had reserved for each of them. It was now time for me to do me.

About the Author

Originally sentenced to four hundred and eighty months [40 years] in Federal prison for being part of a 9 state drug conspiracy, ShaKim Bio traveled to 8 maximum Federal penitentiaries.

Throughout his journey he earned his G.E.D. and numerous certificates from taking classes and courses.

He is the author of 3 novels - *Love, Hell or Right*, *The Last Illest*, and *Loyalty, Honor and Respect*. He also writes a monthly column for Gorillaconvict.com titled "S.H.A.K.I.M.'s HOOD."

ShaKim Bio stayed in the law library and gave back time 3 times on the Federal Drug Amendments 706, 750, and most recently 782. He is due for release November 2, 2015, after serving 21 years, 11 months in the Feds. He is currently still at war for his freedom in the State of Ohio.

To contact ShaKim Bio you can reach him at ShaKim_biochemical@yahoo.com

Shakim Bio

SHAKIM BIO
& MIKAHS 7 PUBLISHING PRESENT

LOVE HELL OR RIGHT   **THE OMEGA JON CHRIST- THE LAST ILLEST**   **LOYALTY HONOR & RESPECT**

ALL TITLES AVAILABLE ON AMAZON

"S.h.a.k.i.m.'s Hood" blog / interviews available at
gorillaconvict.com

 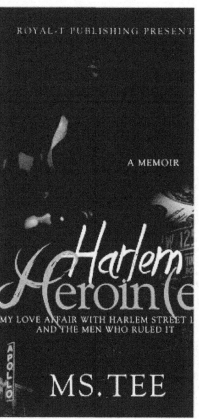

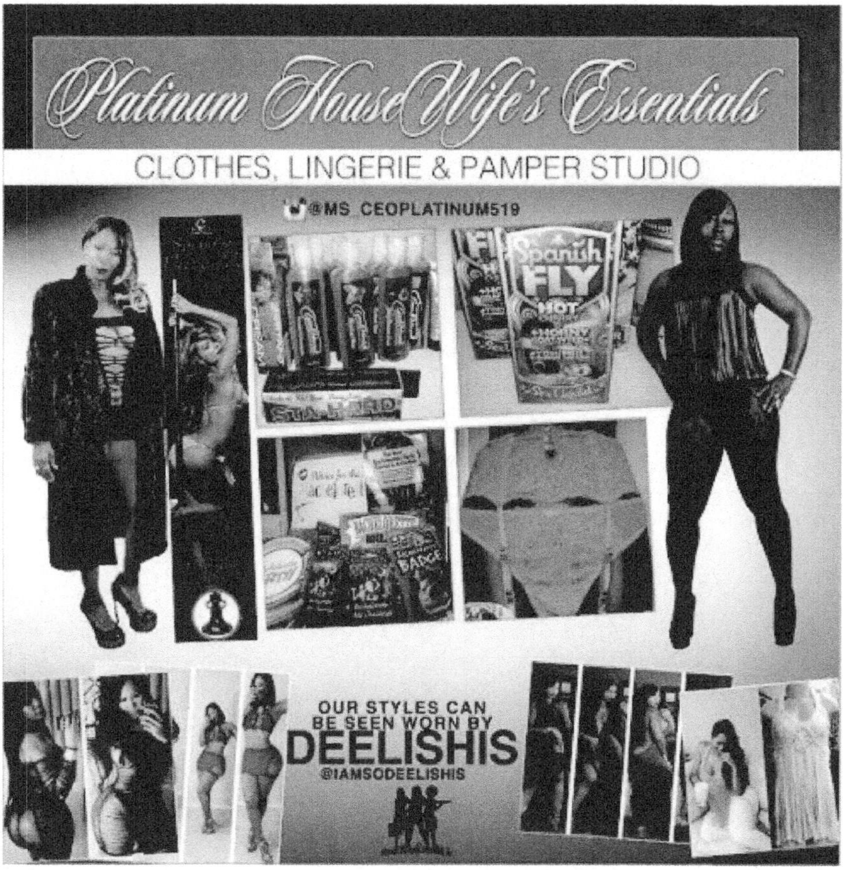
Platinum HouseWife's Essentials
CLOTHES, LINGERIE & PAMPER STUDIO
@MS_CEOPLATINUM519
Spanish FLY
HOT
OUR STYLES CAN BE SEEN WORN BY
DEELISHIS
@IAMSODEELISHIS

Made in the USA
Coppell, TX
08 February 2022

73149204R00134